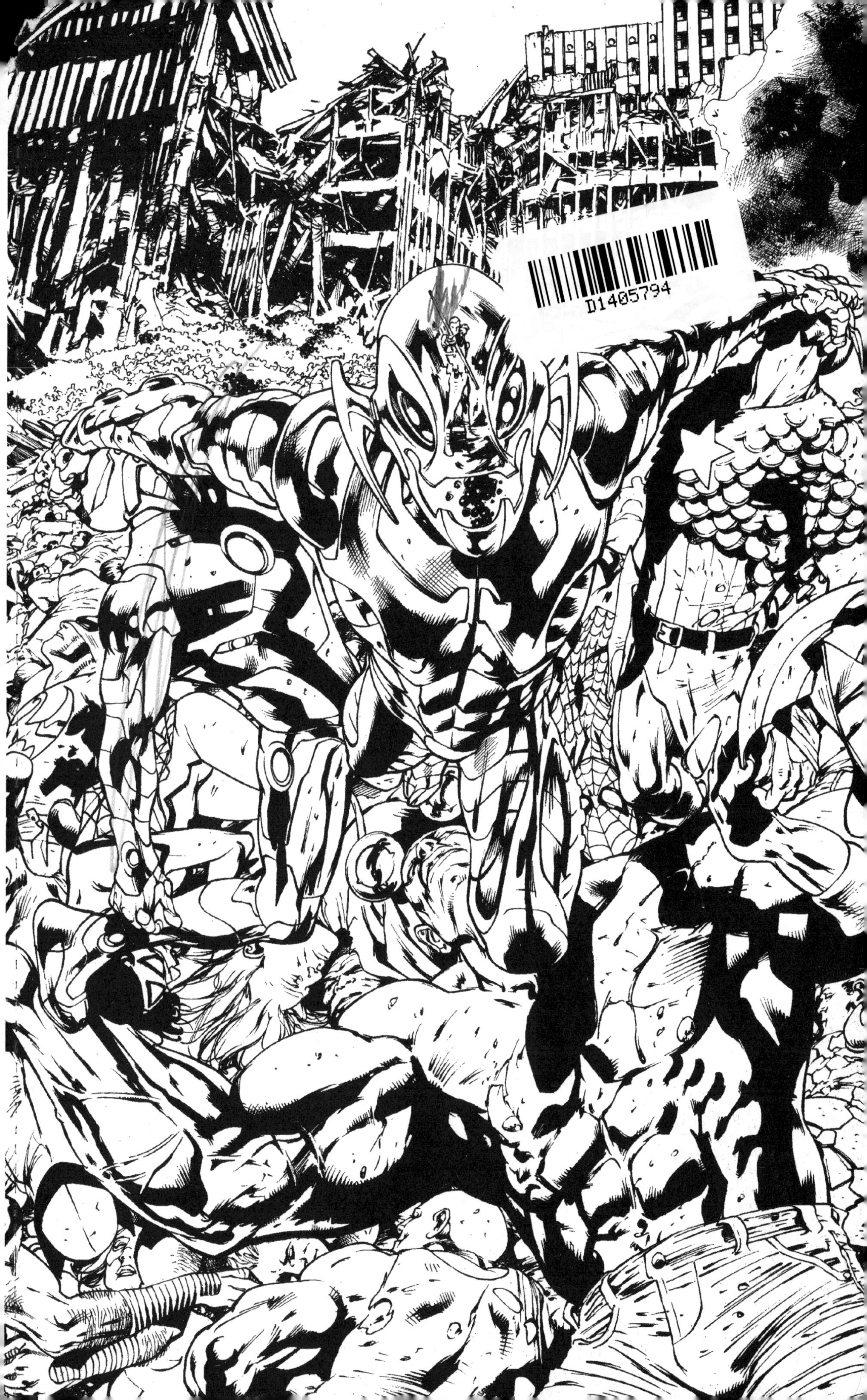

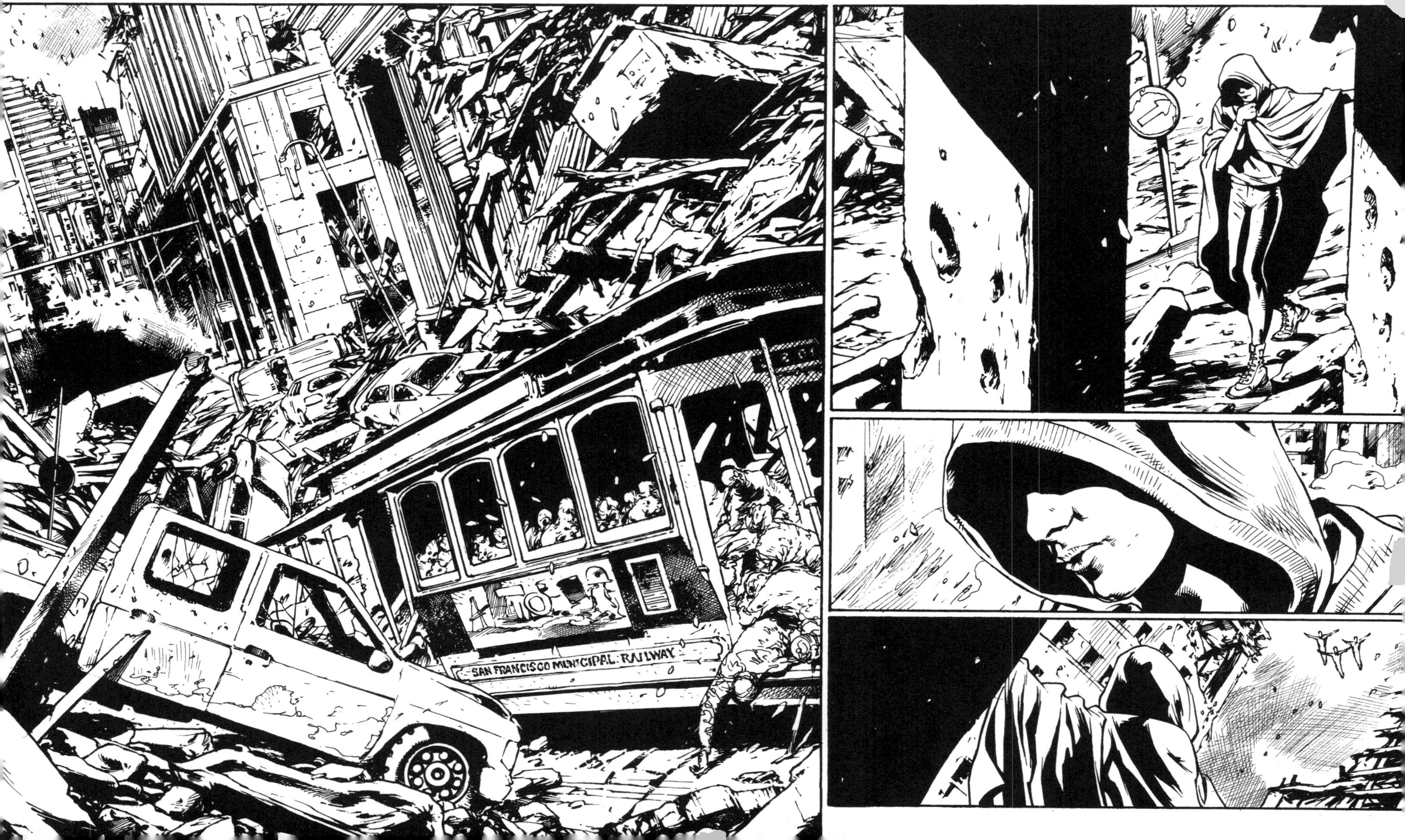
SAN FRANCISCO MUNICIPAL RAILWAY

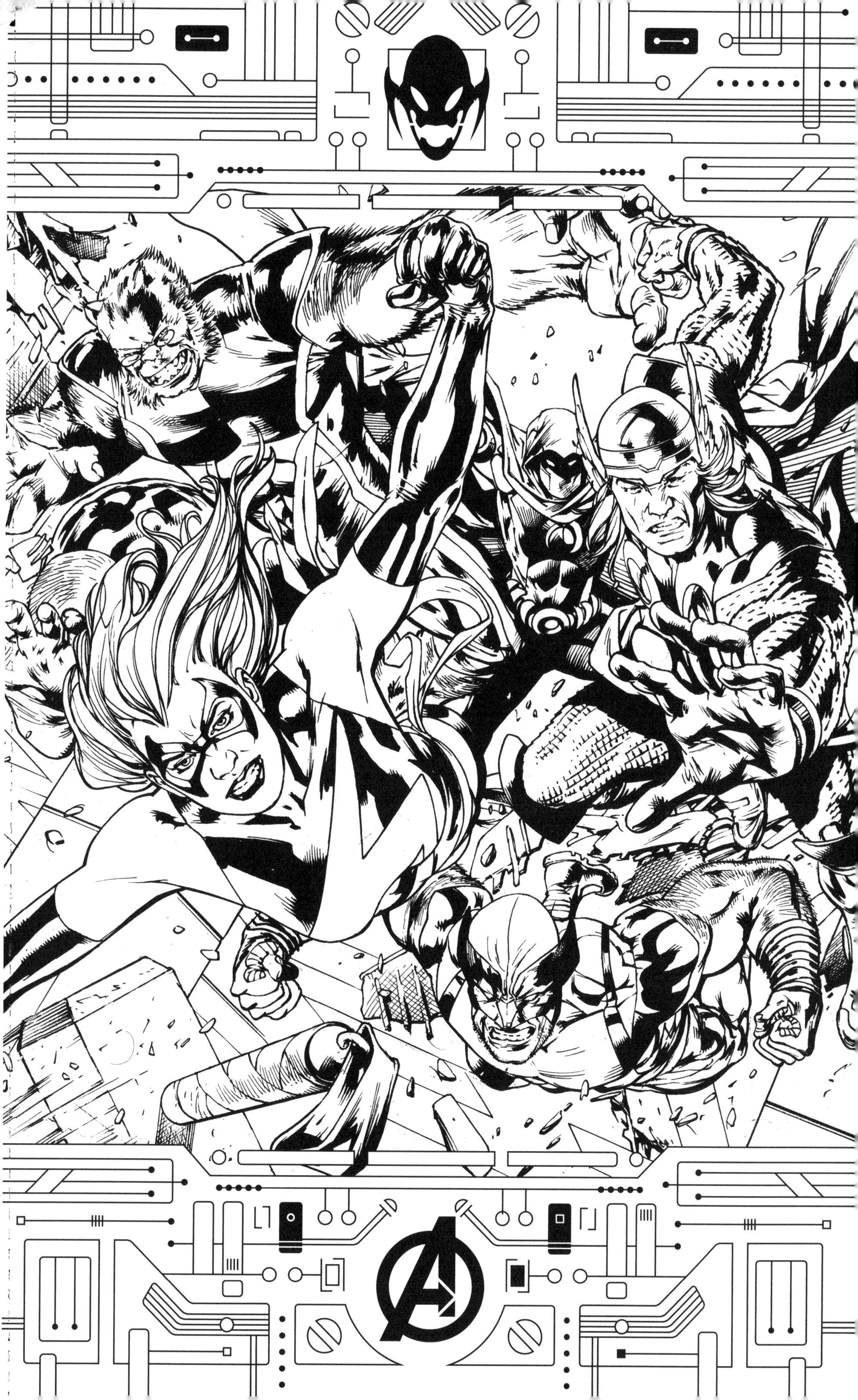

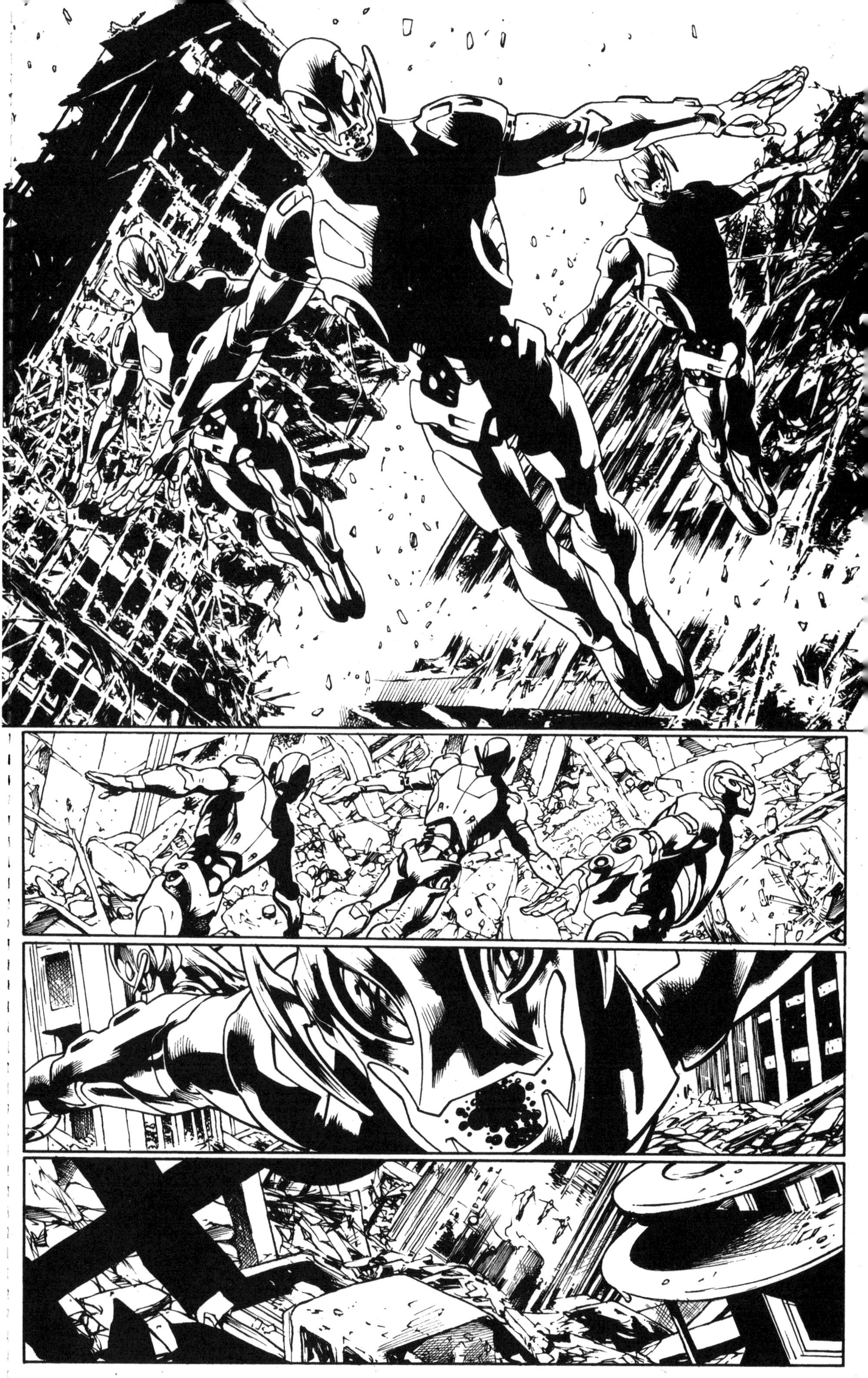

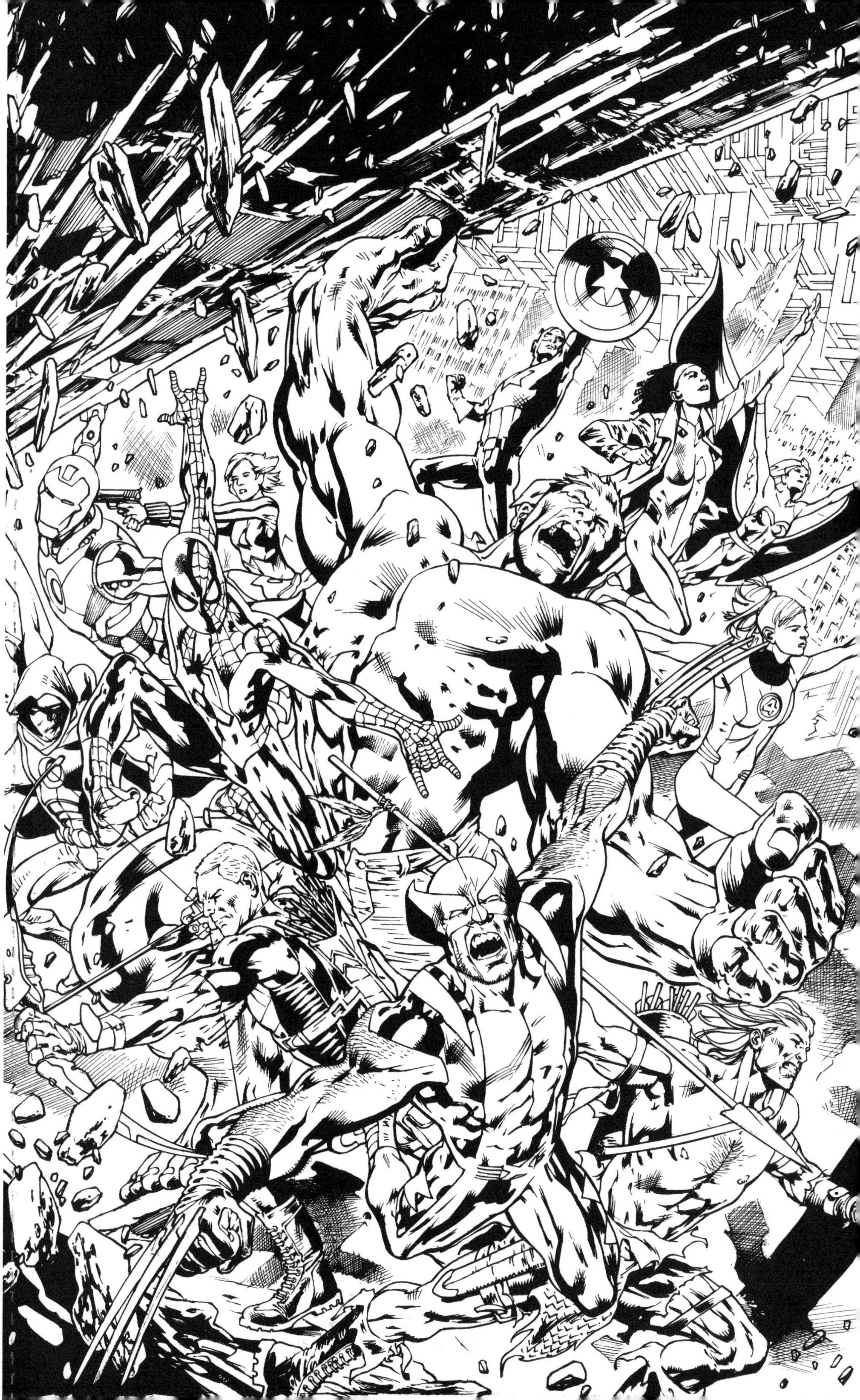

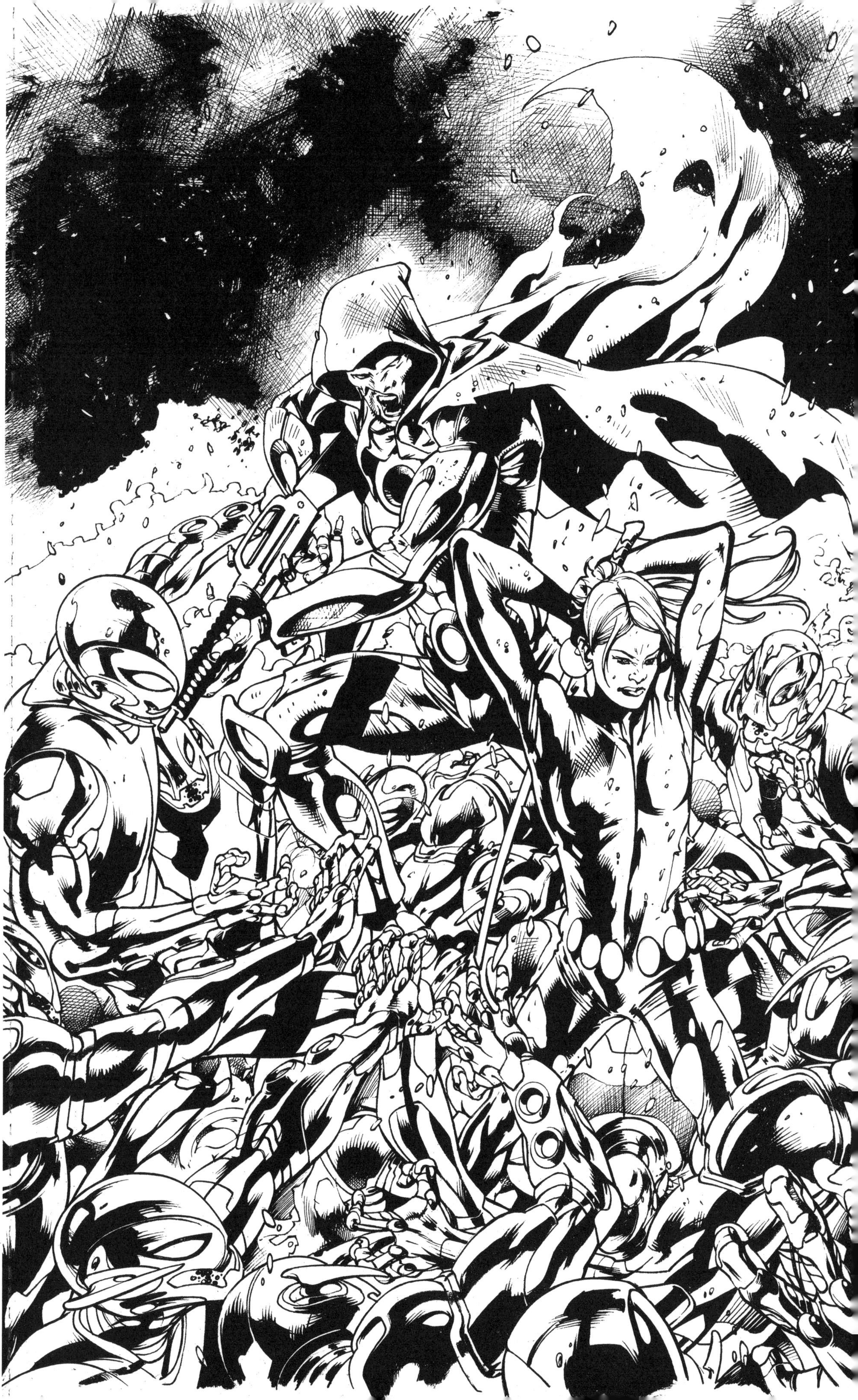

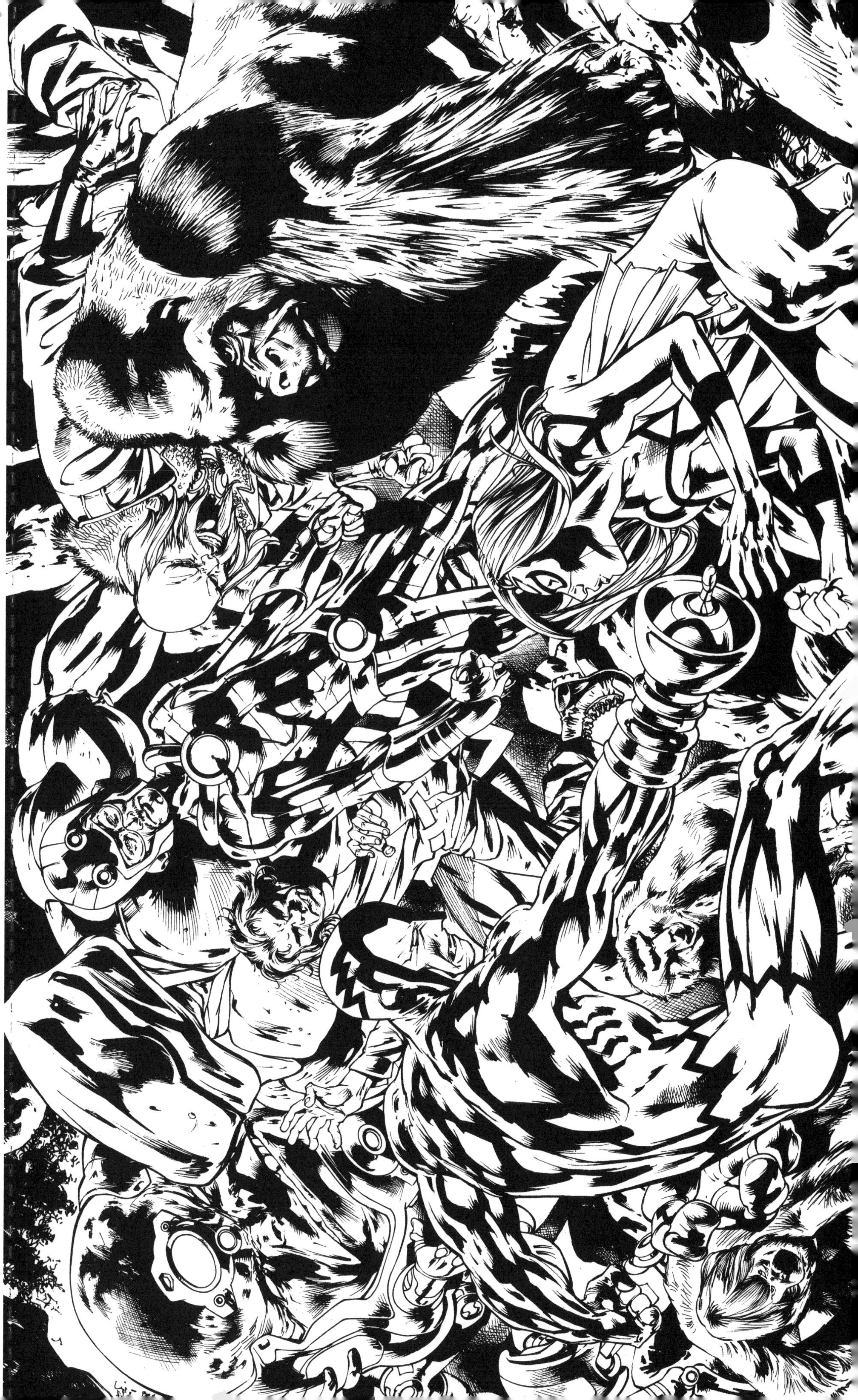

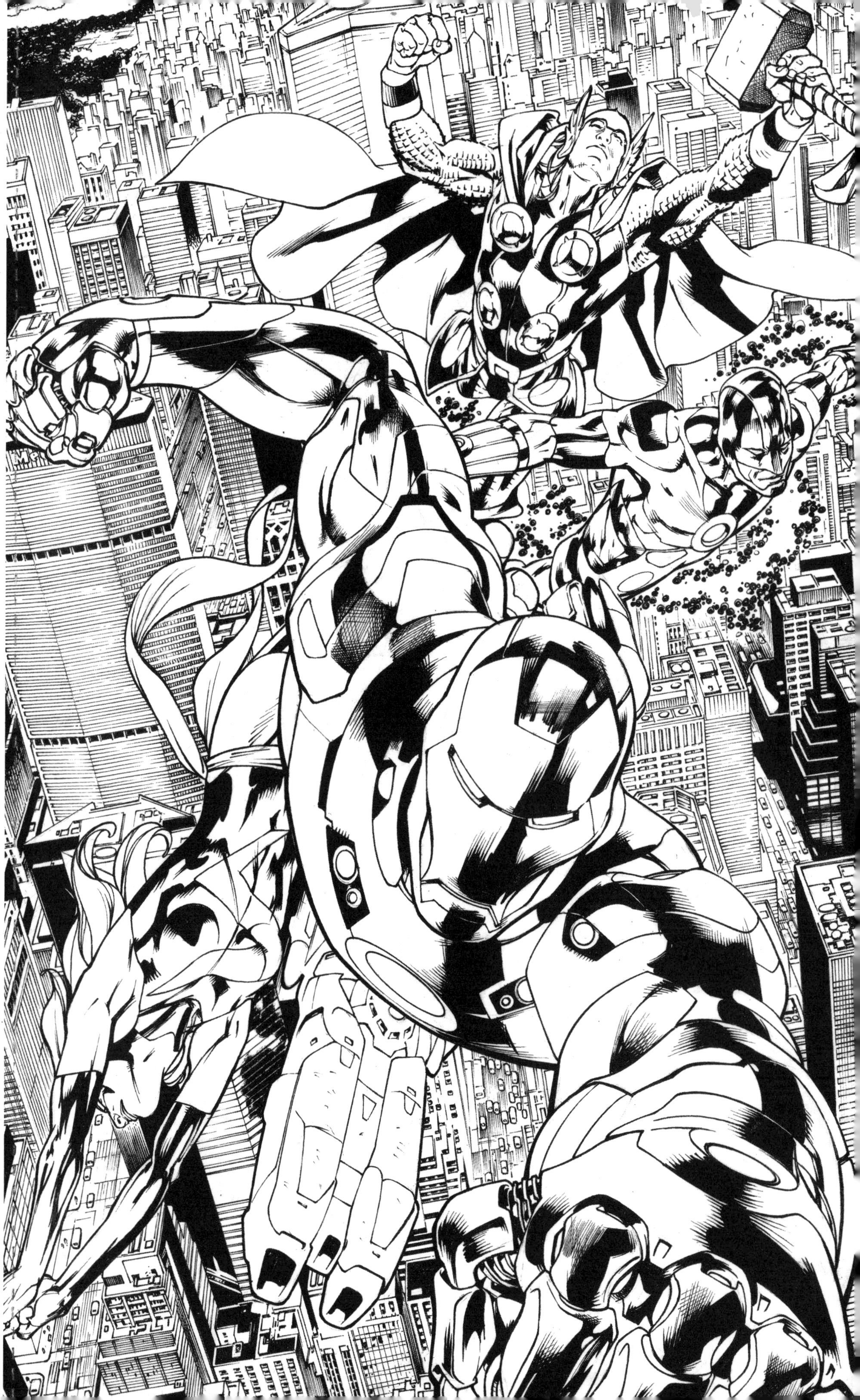

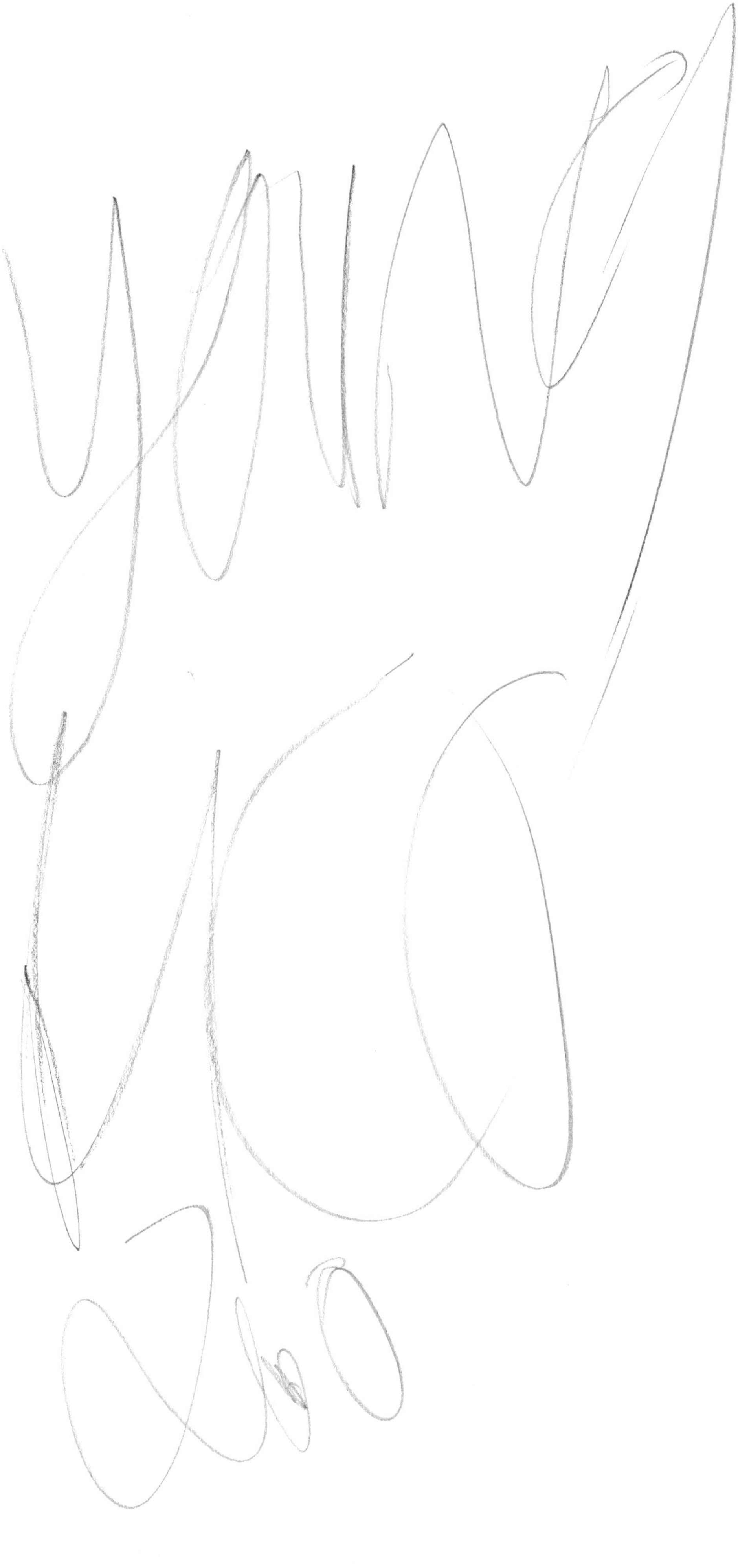

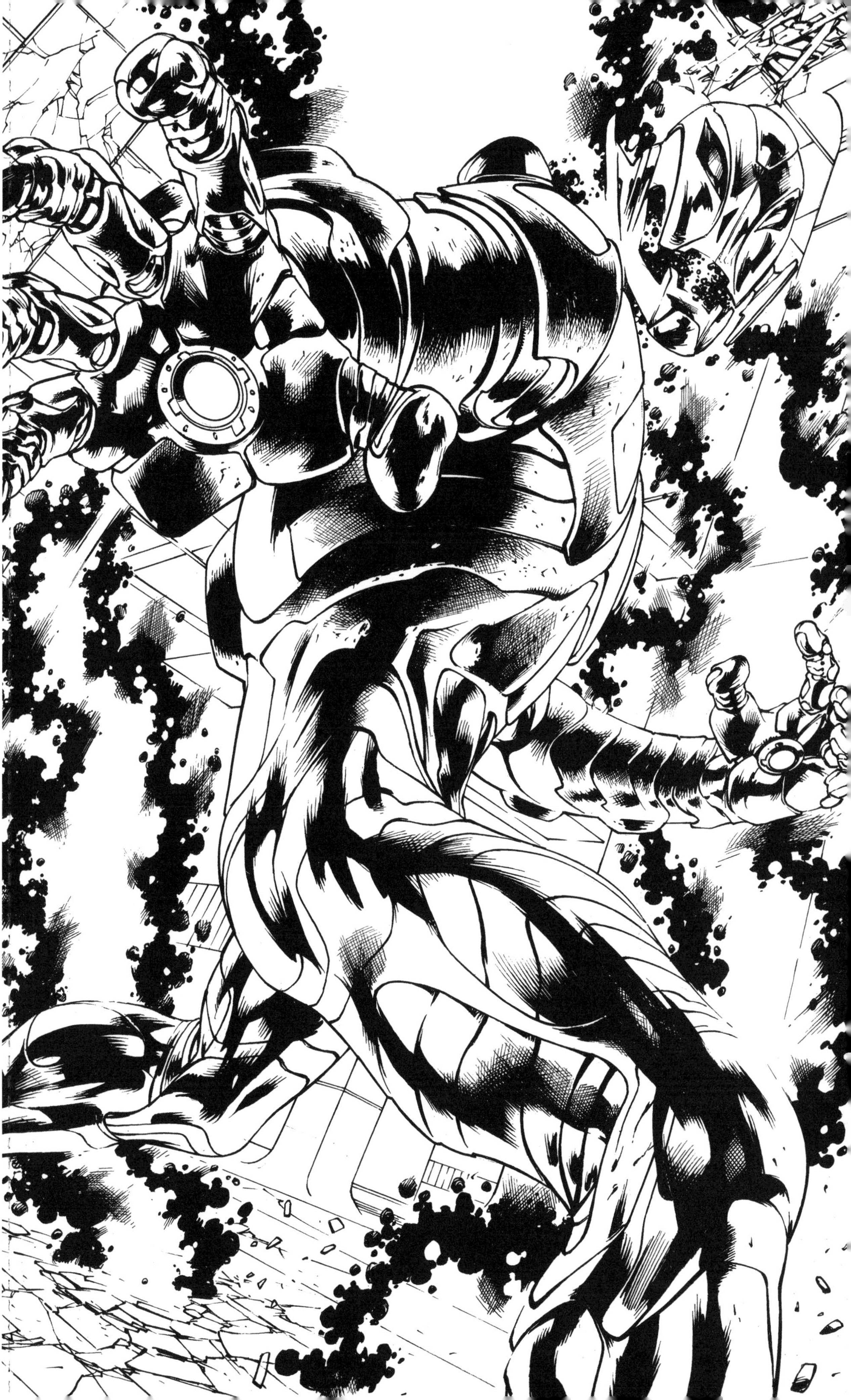

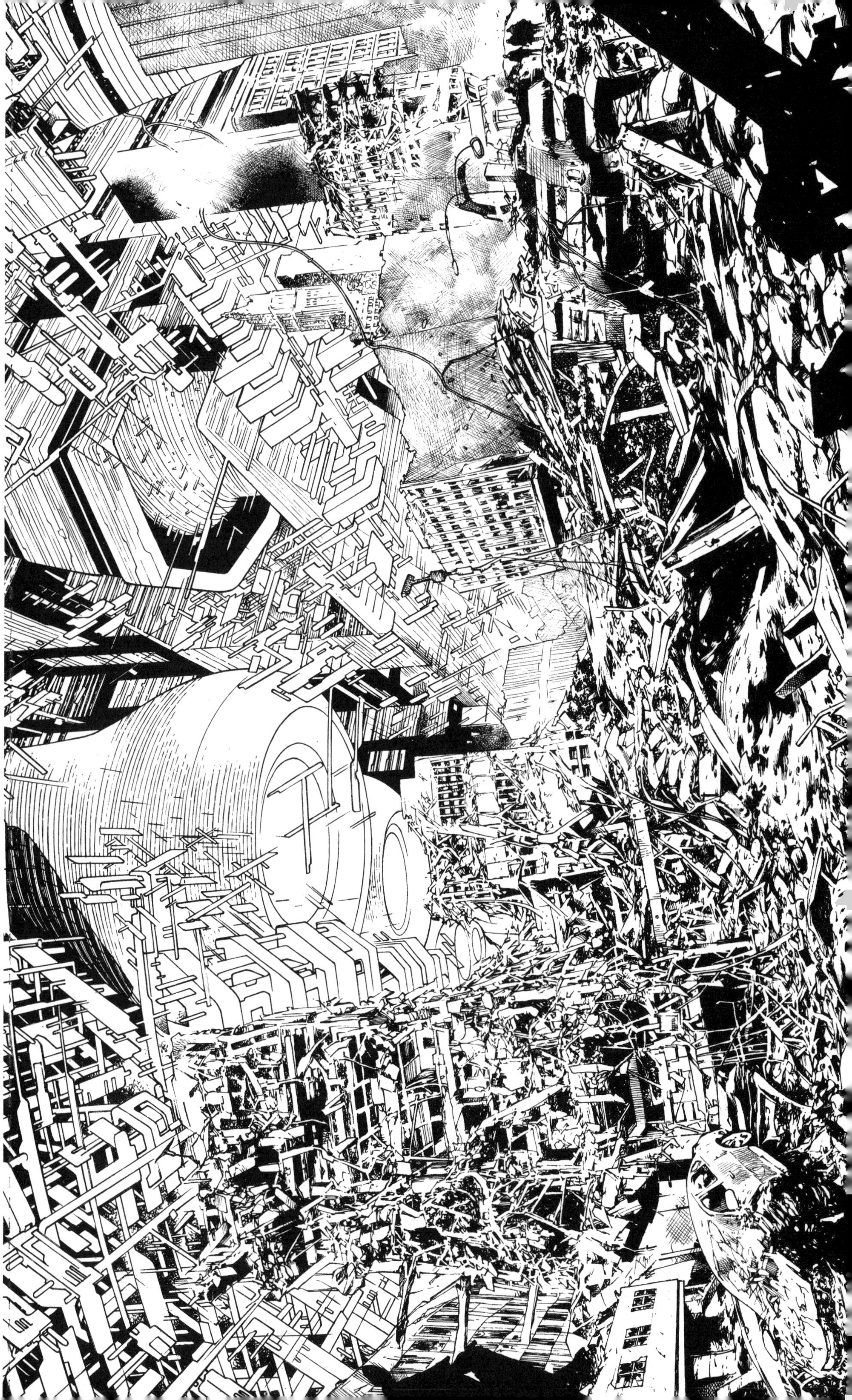

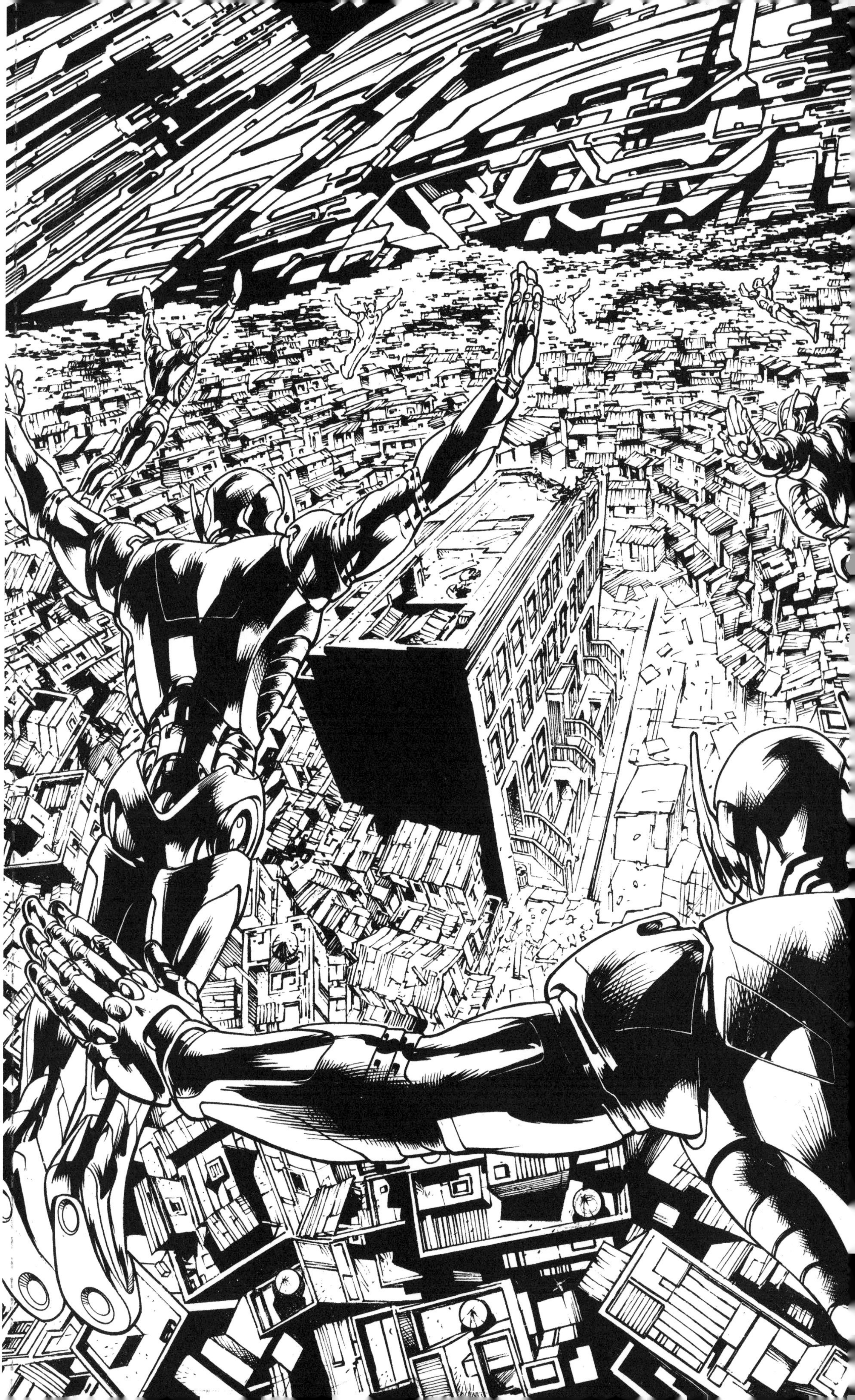

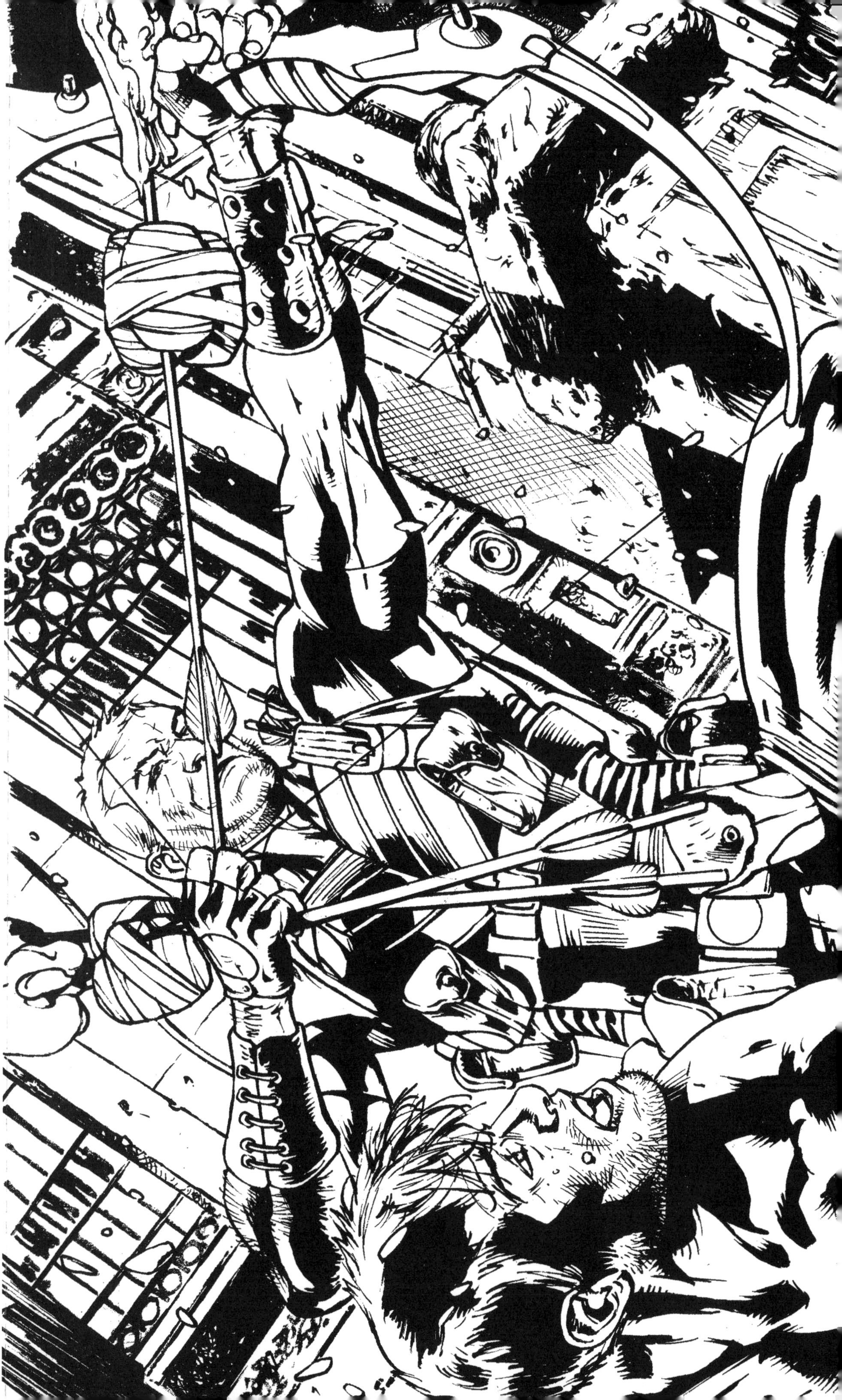

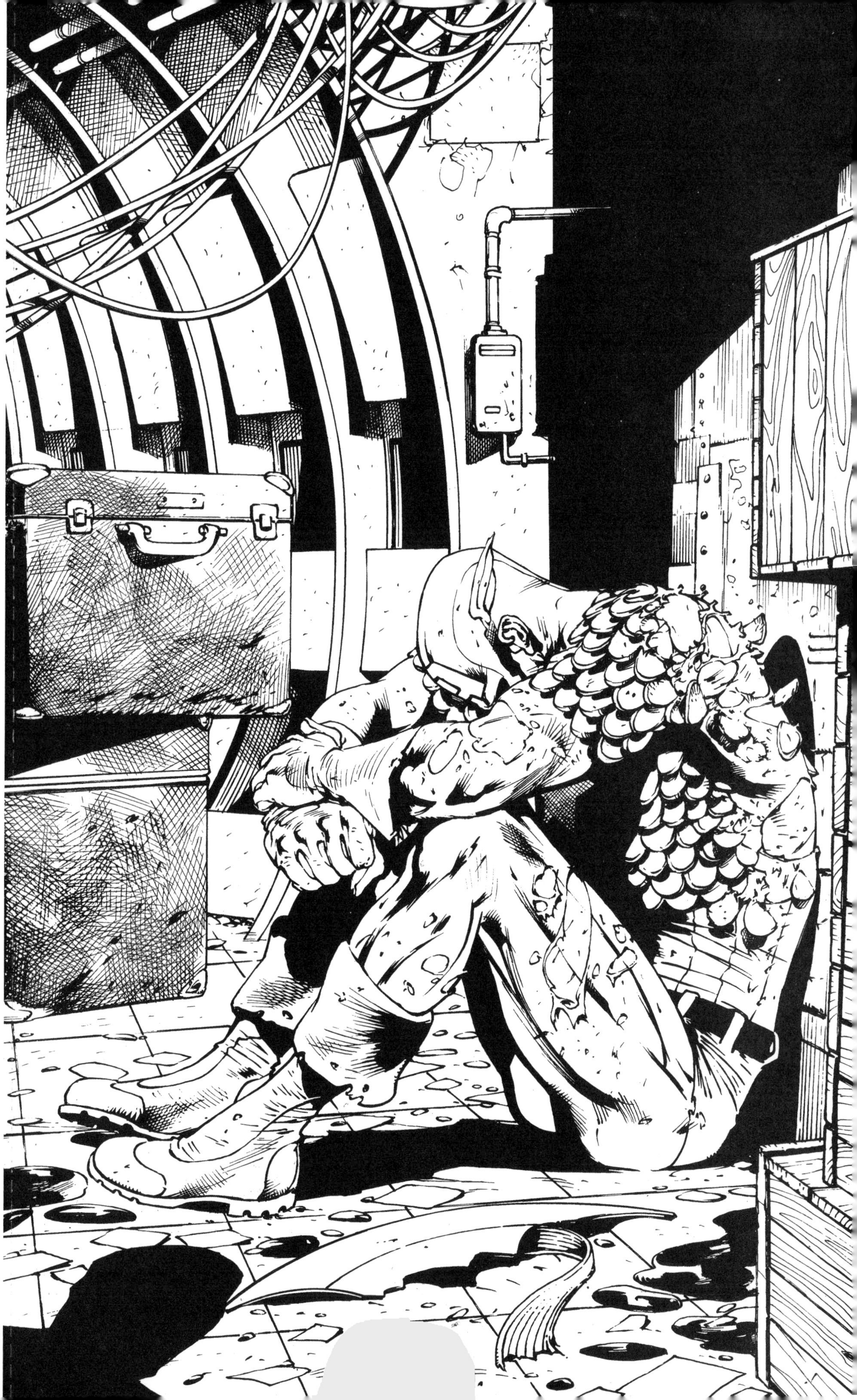

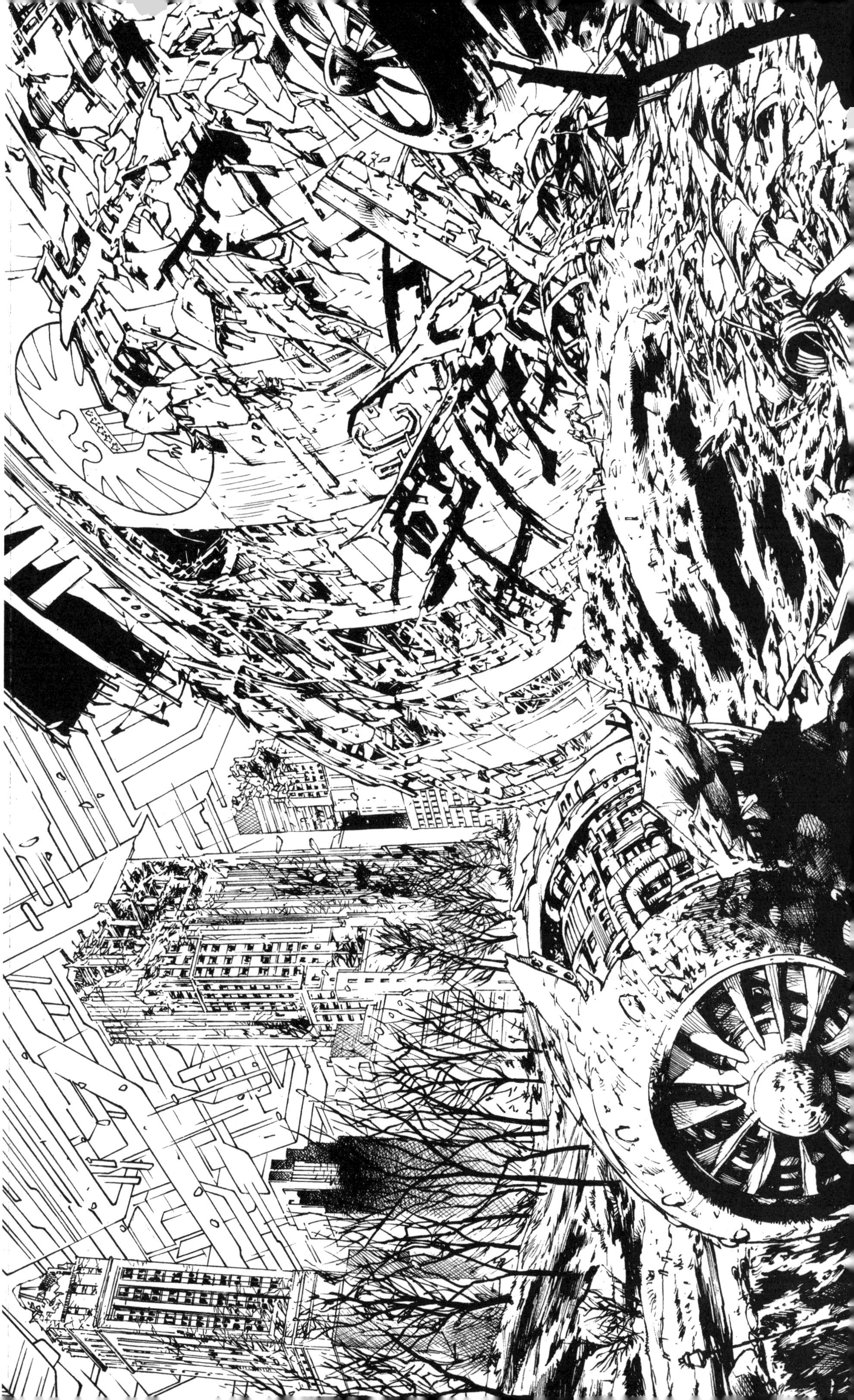

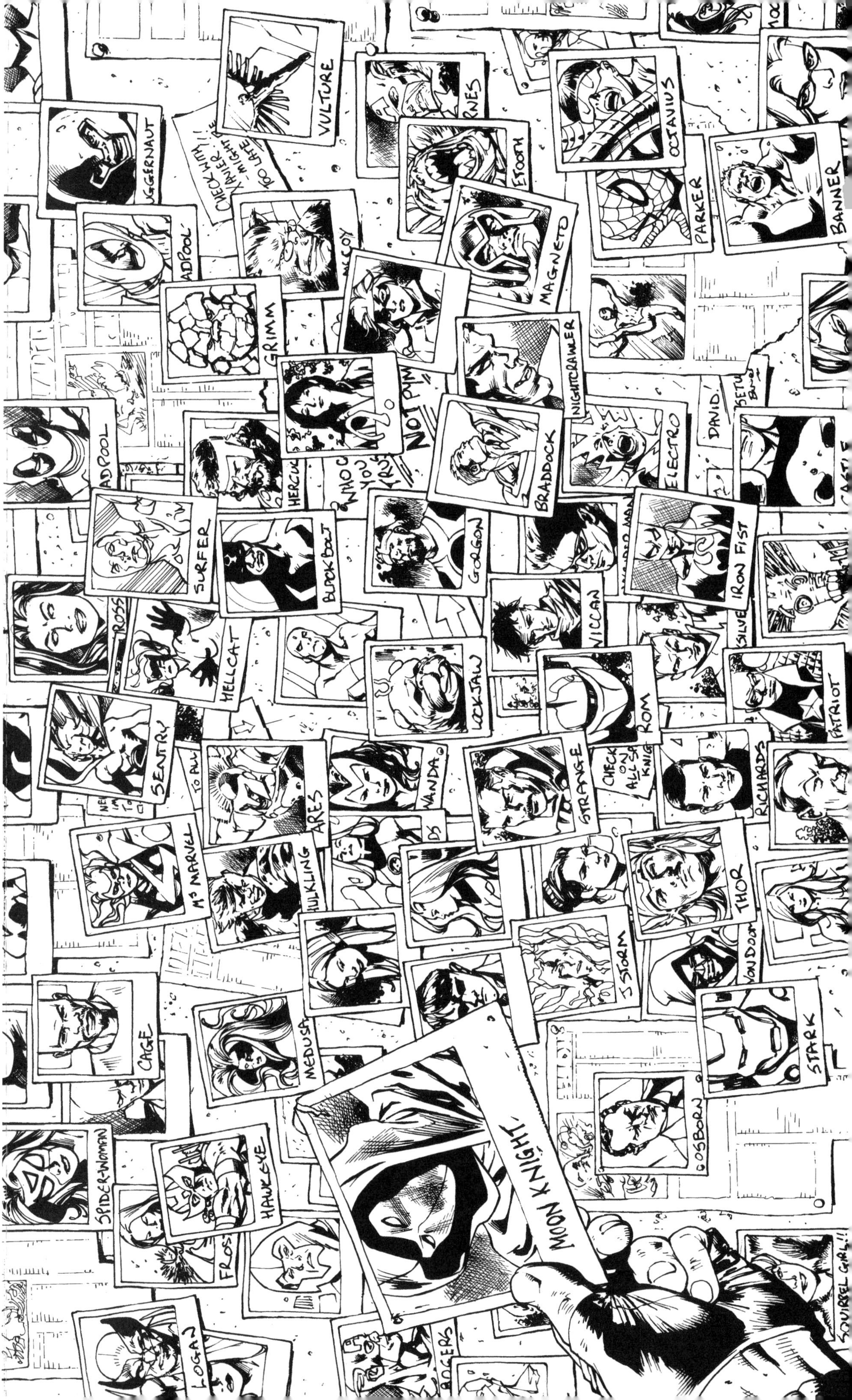

VULTURE
OCTAVIUS
MAGNETO
PARKER
BANNER
GRIMM
NIGHTCRAWLER
NOT PYM
BRADDOCK
ELECTRO
DAVID
SURFER
BLACK BOLT
GORGON
IRON FIST
WICCAN
ROSS
HELLCAT
LOCKJAW
ROM
PATRIOT
SENTRY
ARES
WANDA
STRANGE
RICHARDS
Ms MARVEL
HULKLING
THOR
J STORM
VON DOOM
MEDUSA
CAGE
STARK
OSBORN
MOON KNIGHT
SPIDER-WOMAN
HAWKEYE
LOGAN
ROGERS
SQUIRREL GIRL!!

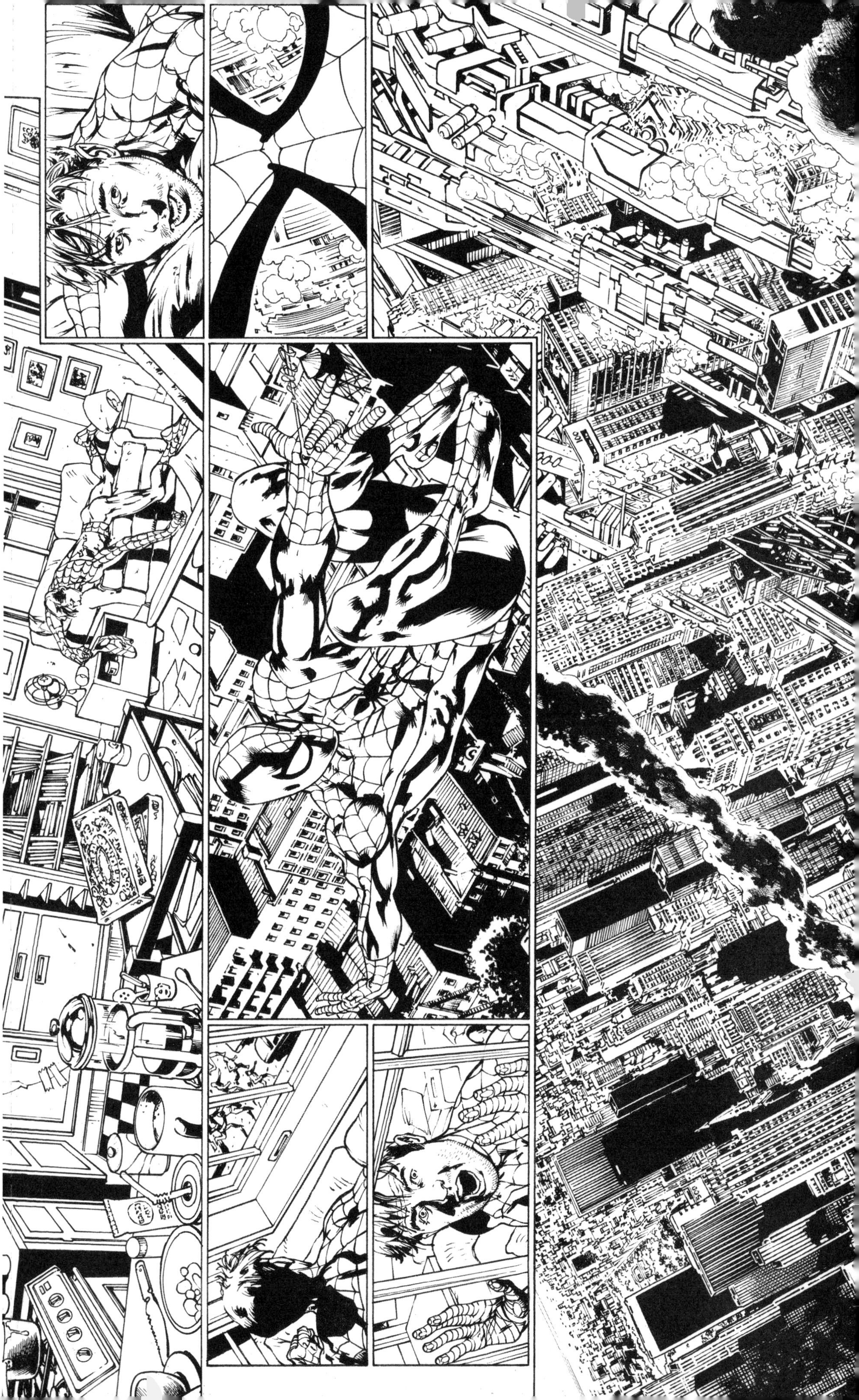

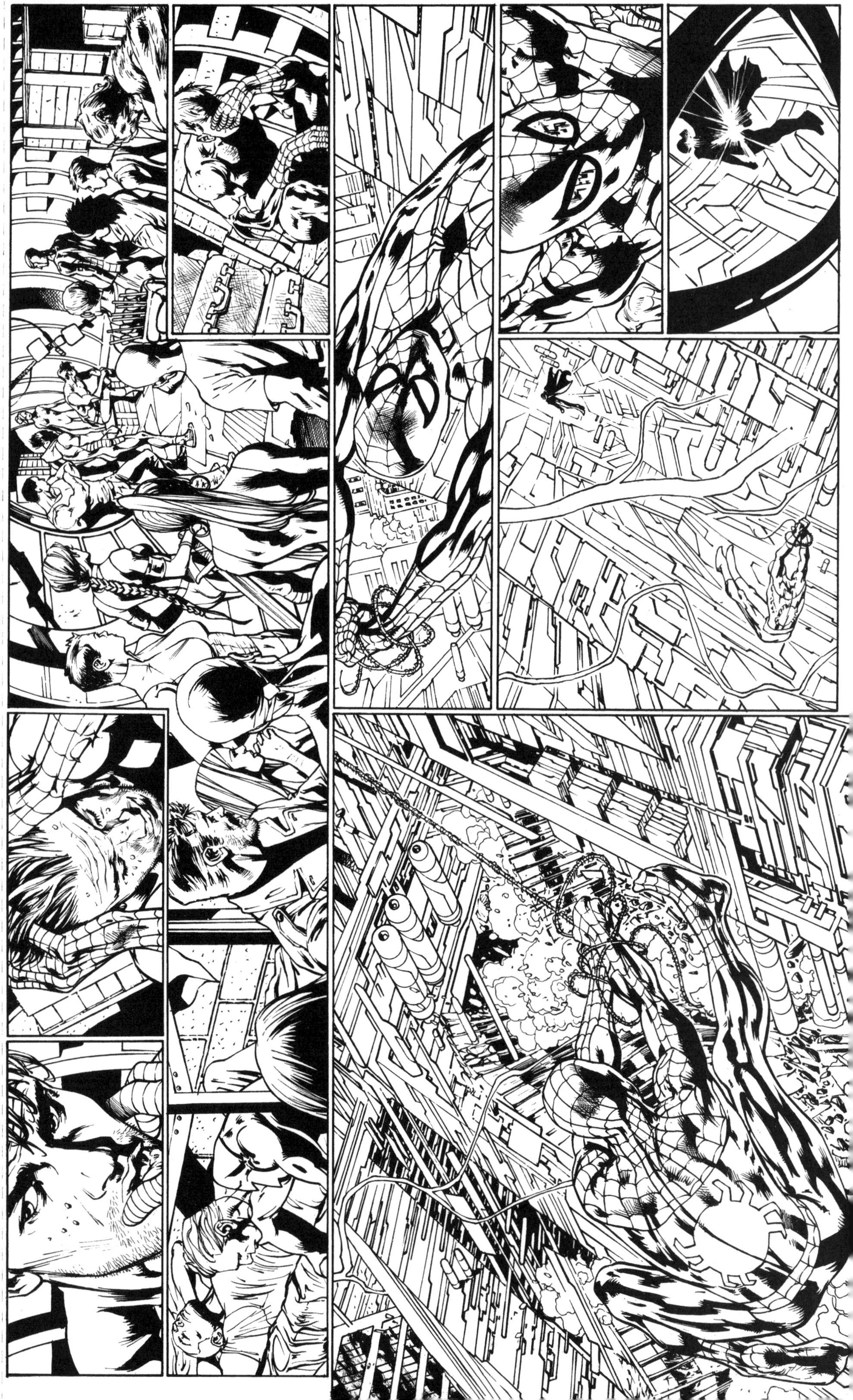

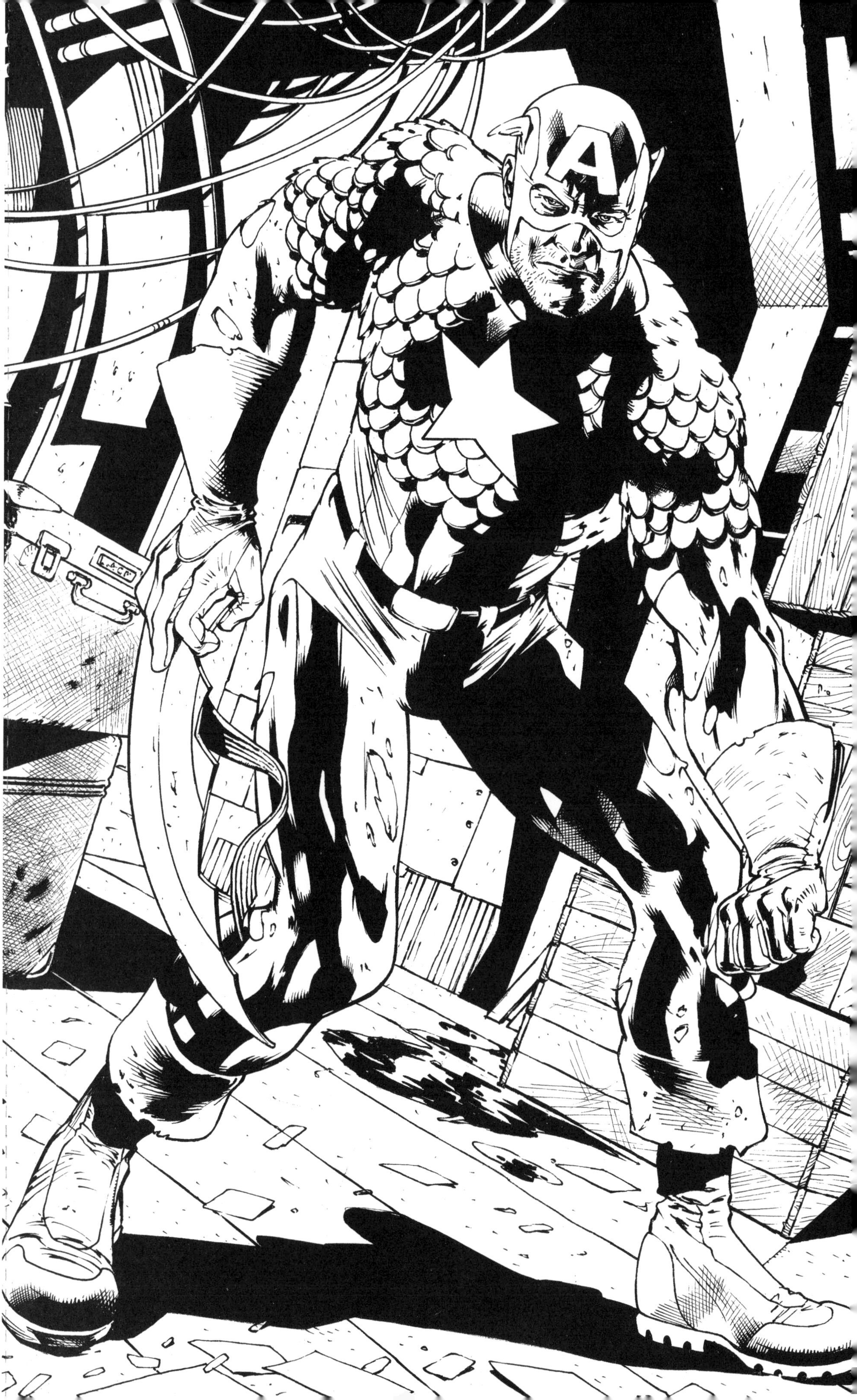

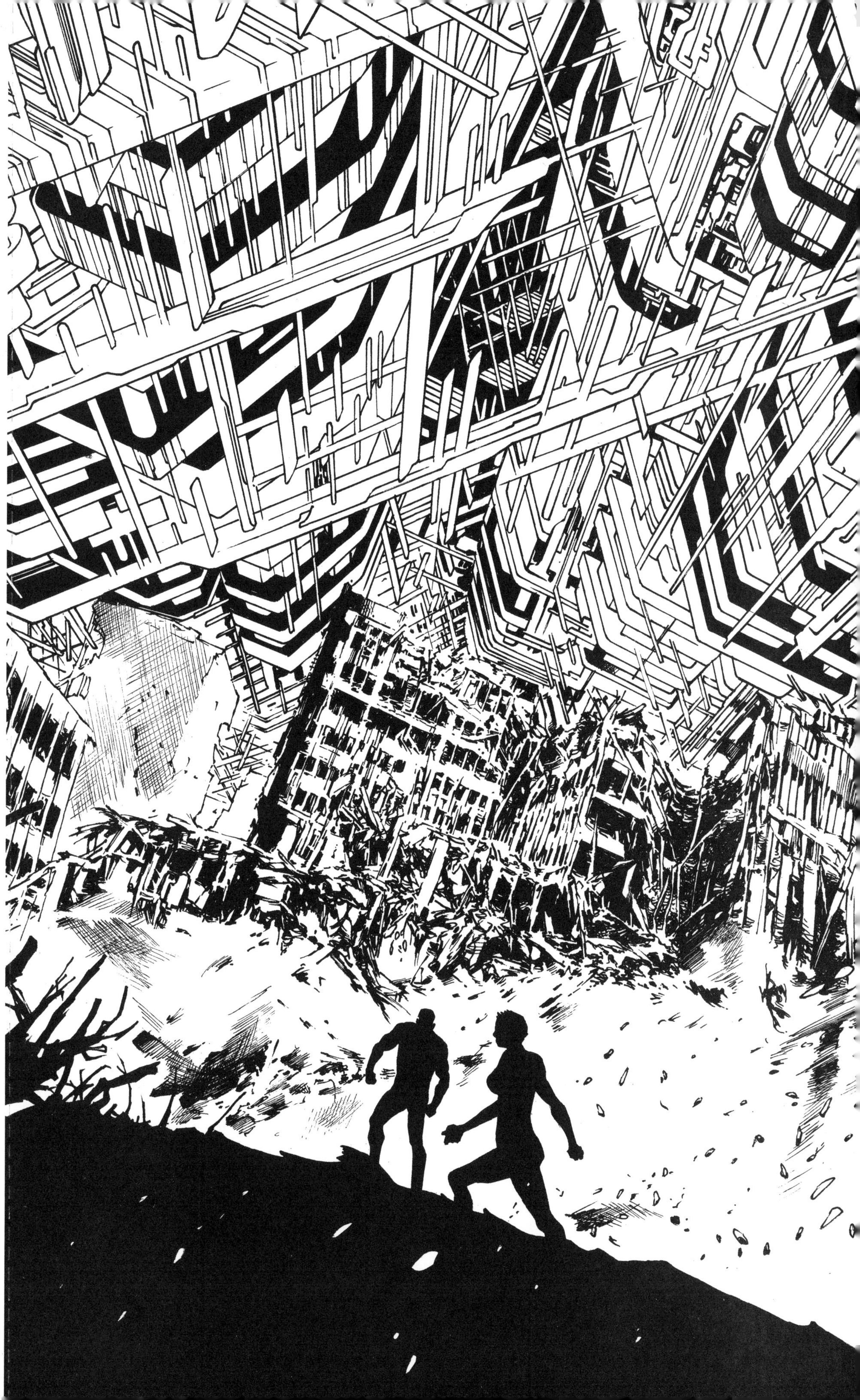

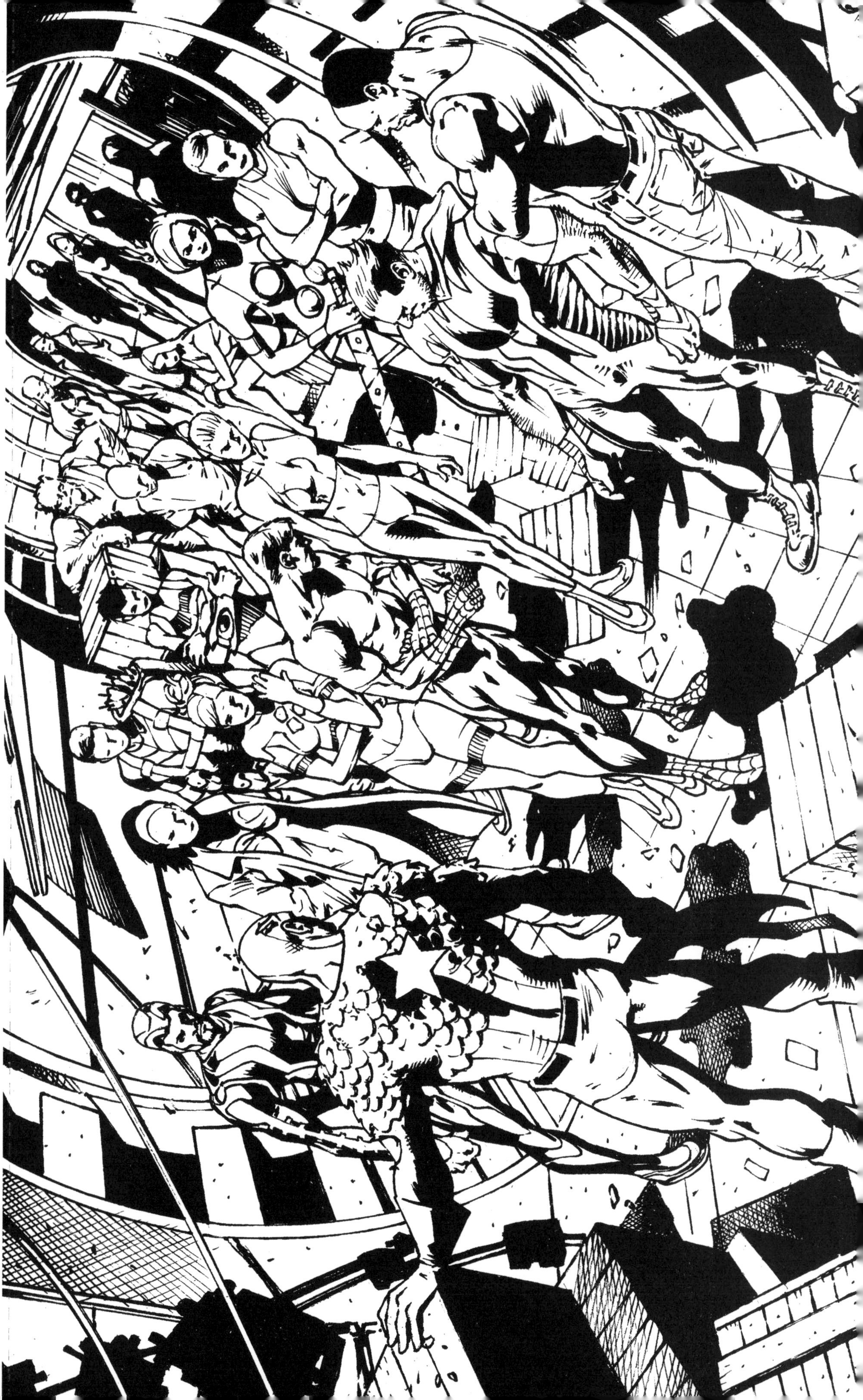

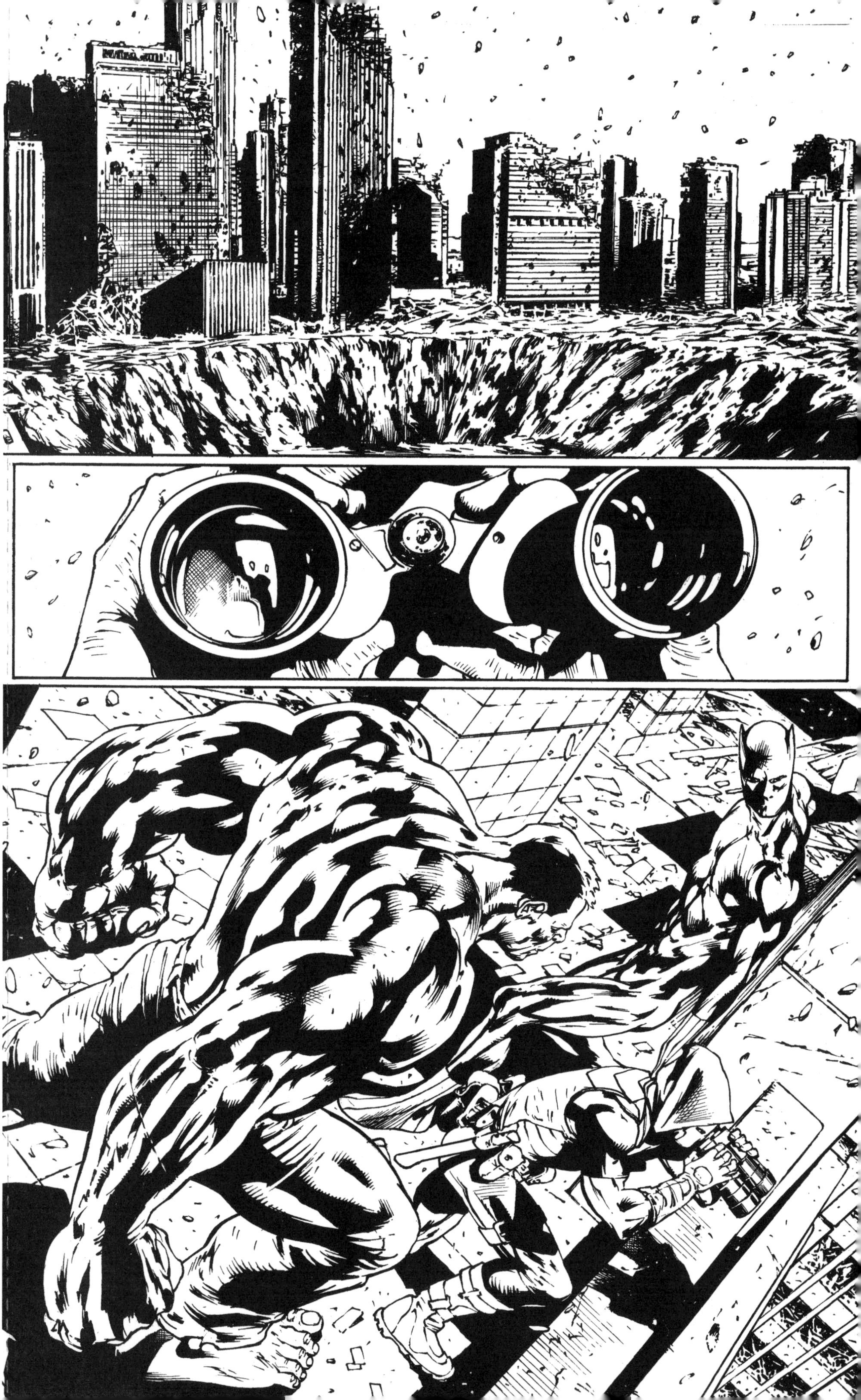

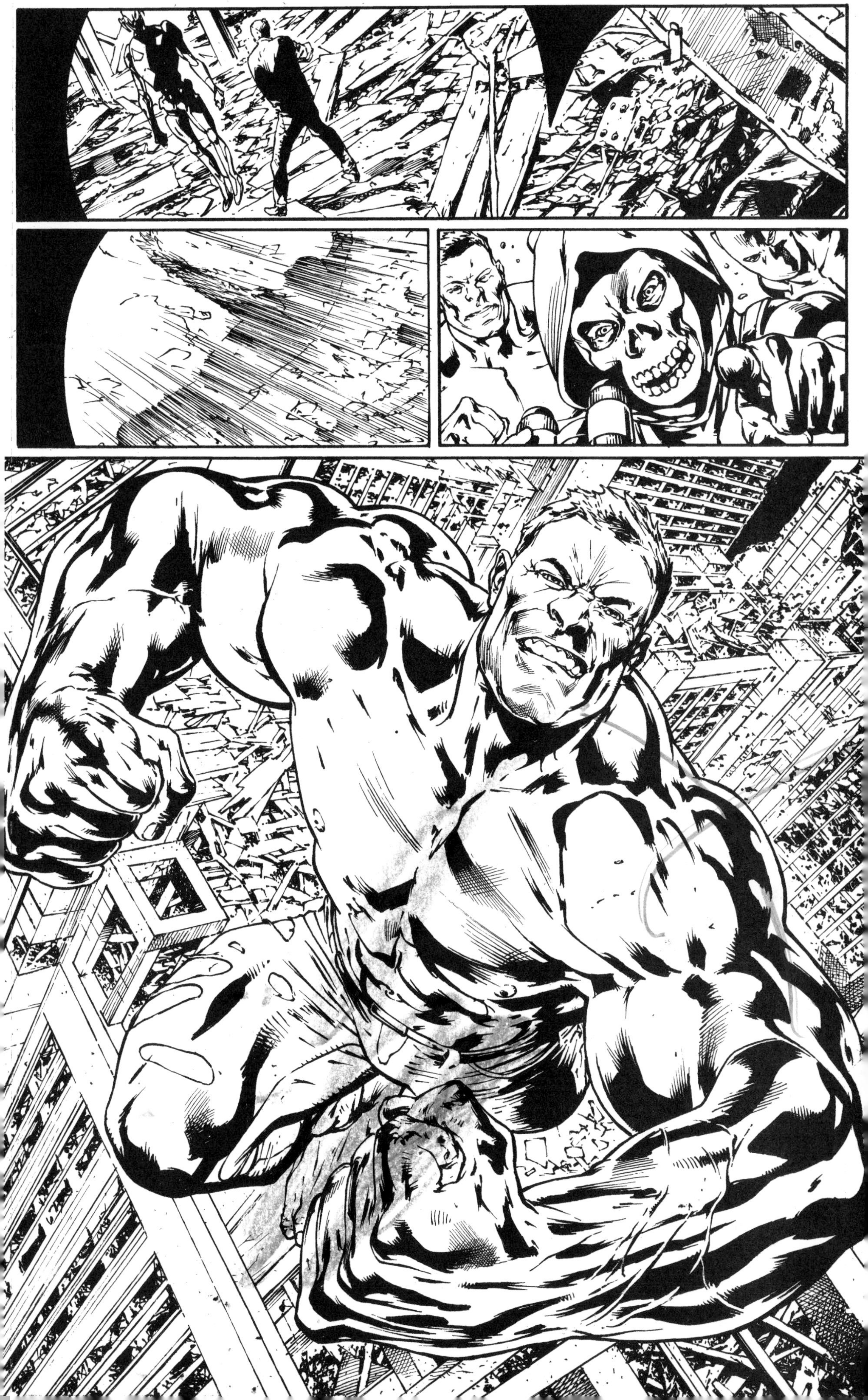

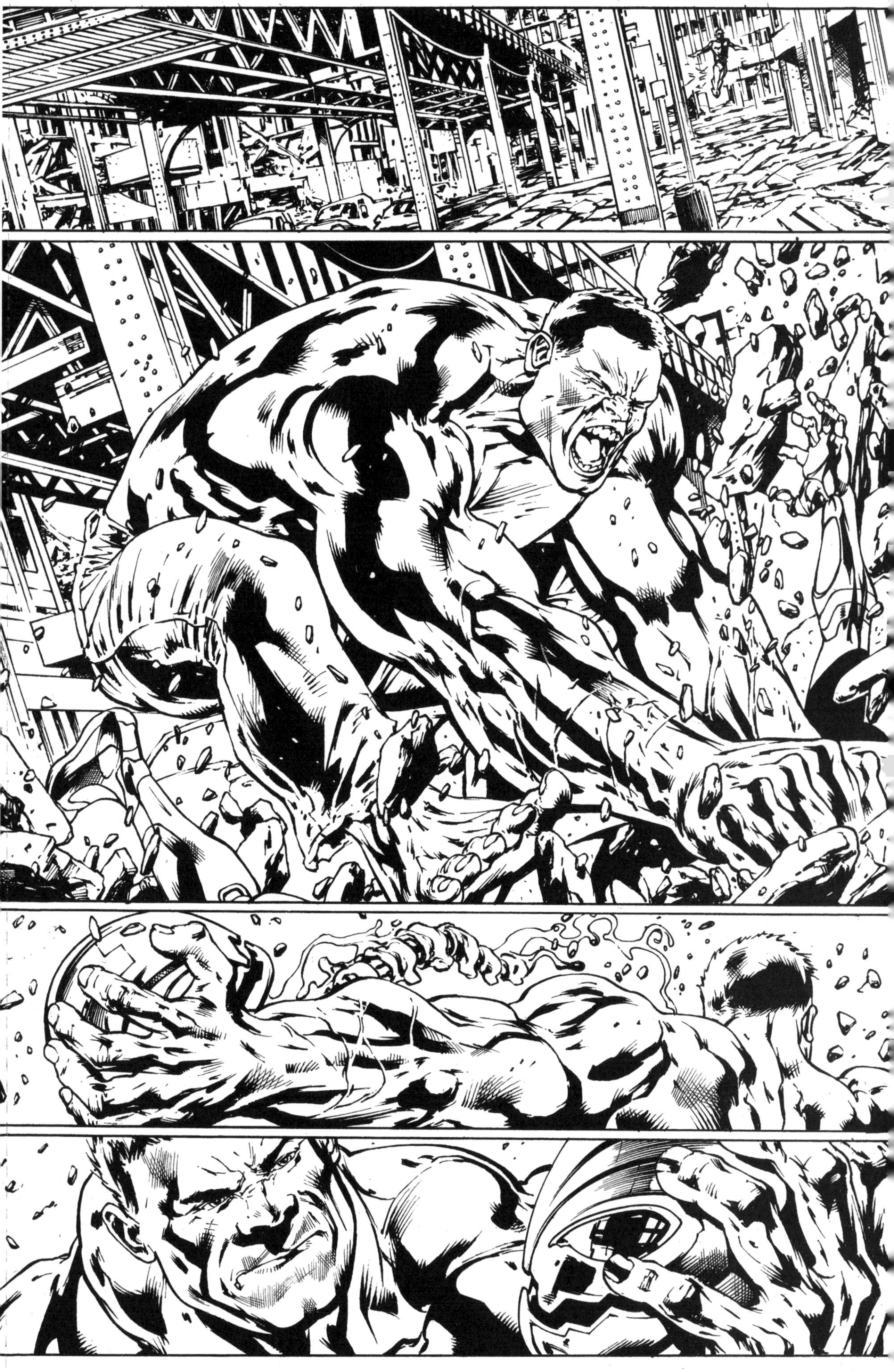

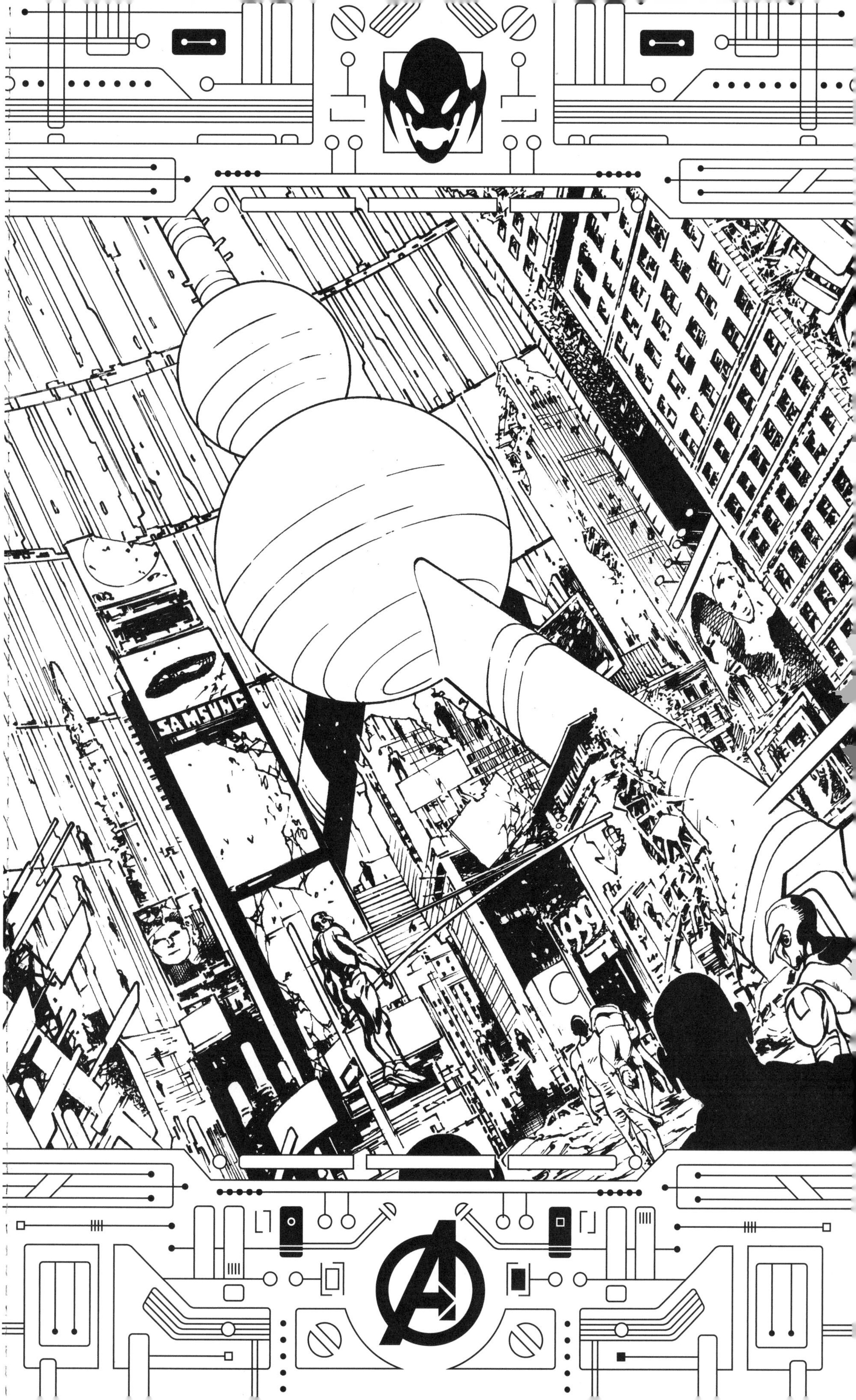
SAMSUNG

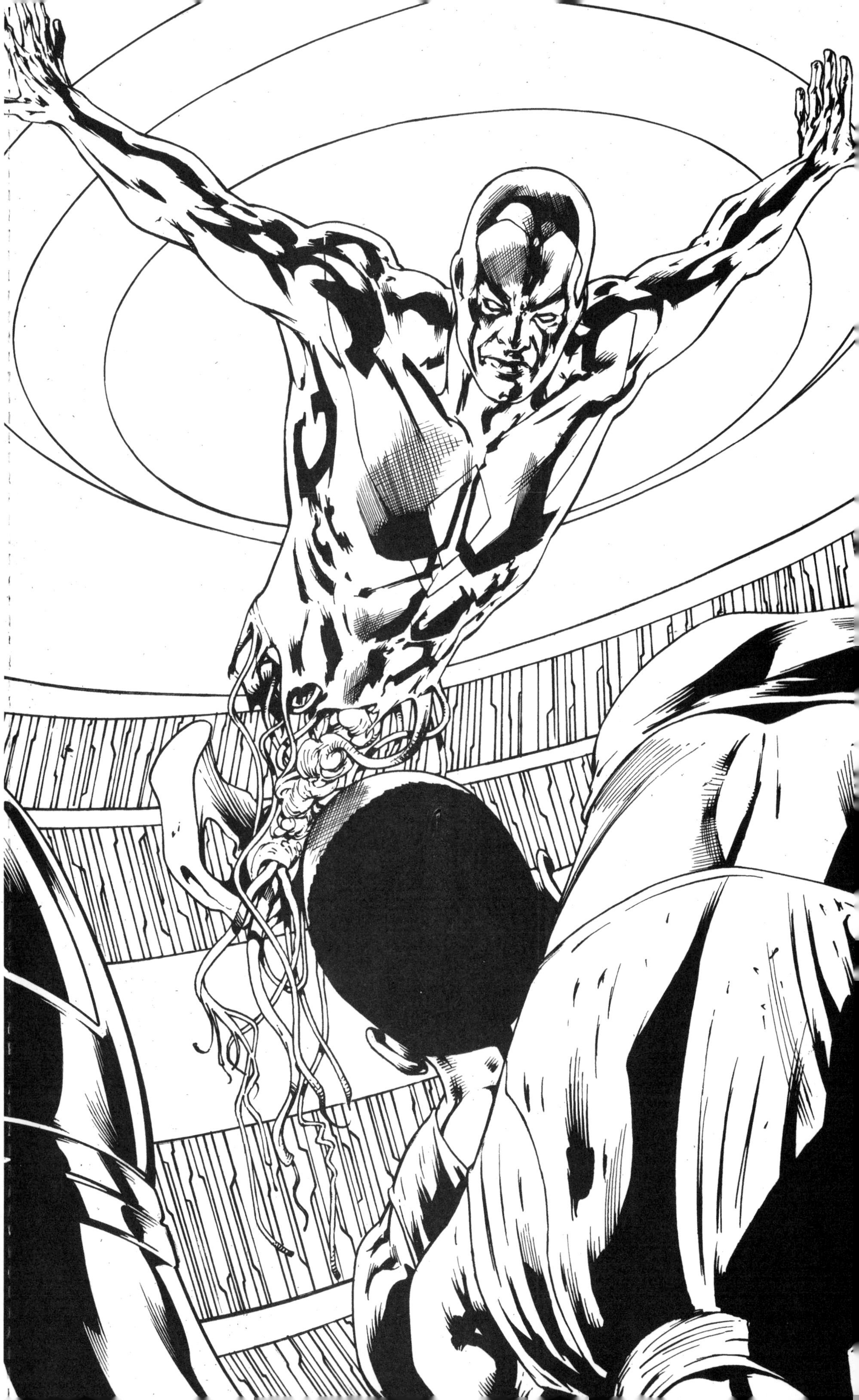

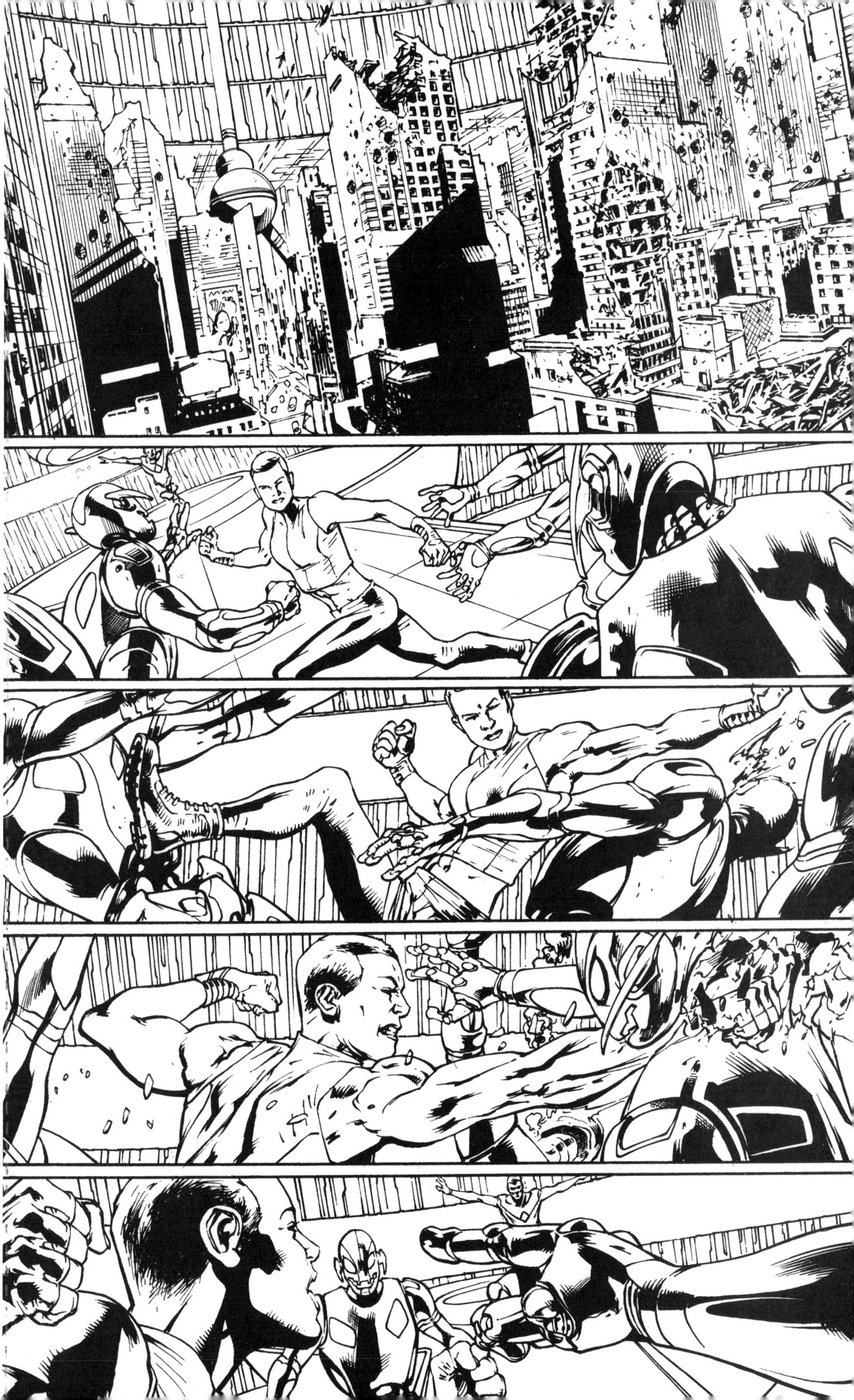

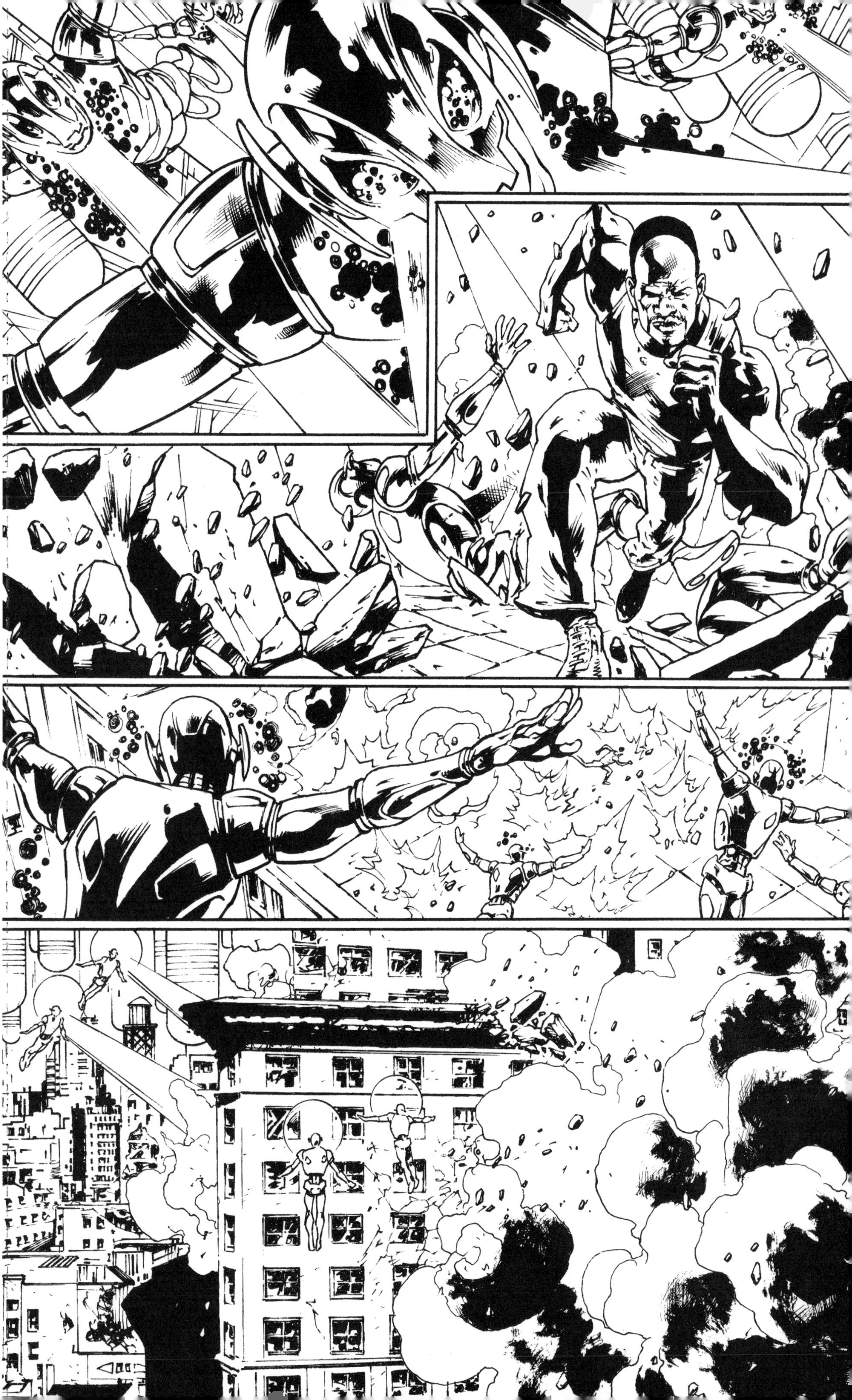

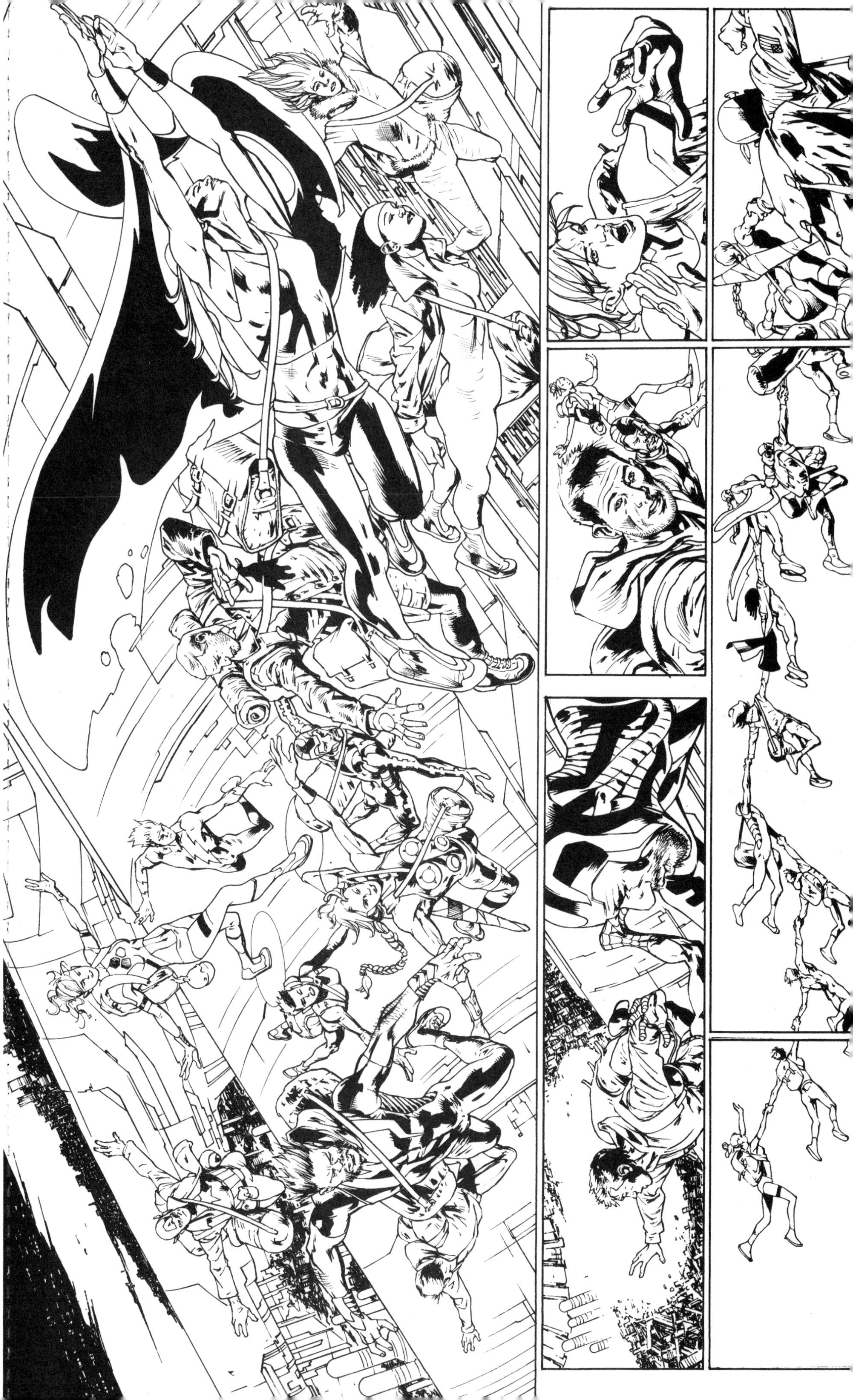

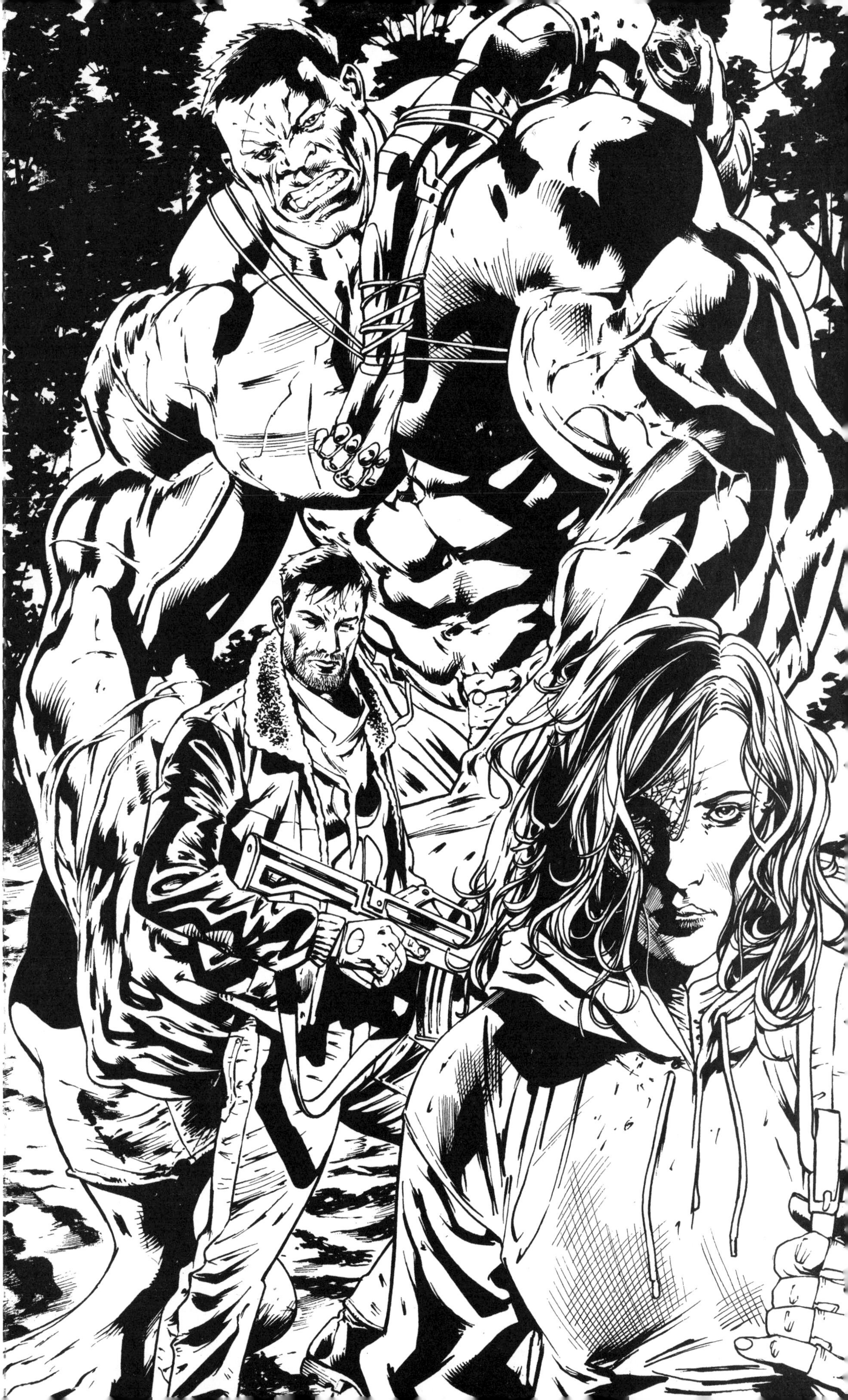

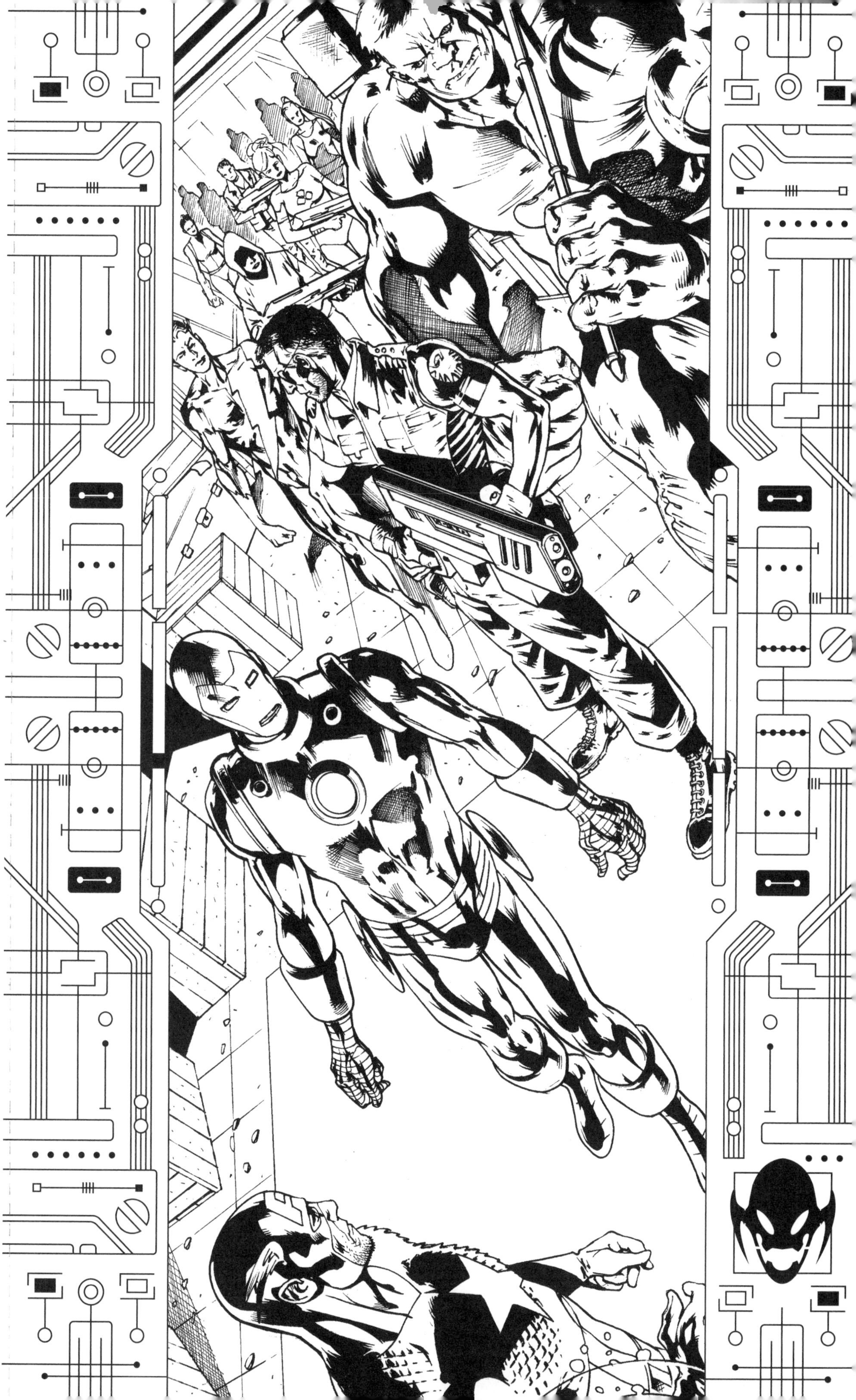

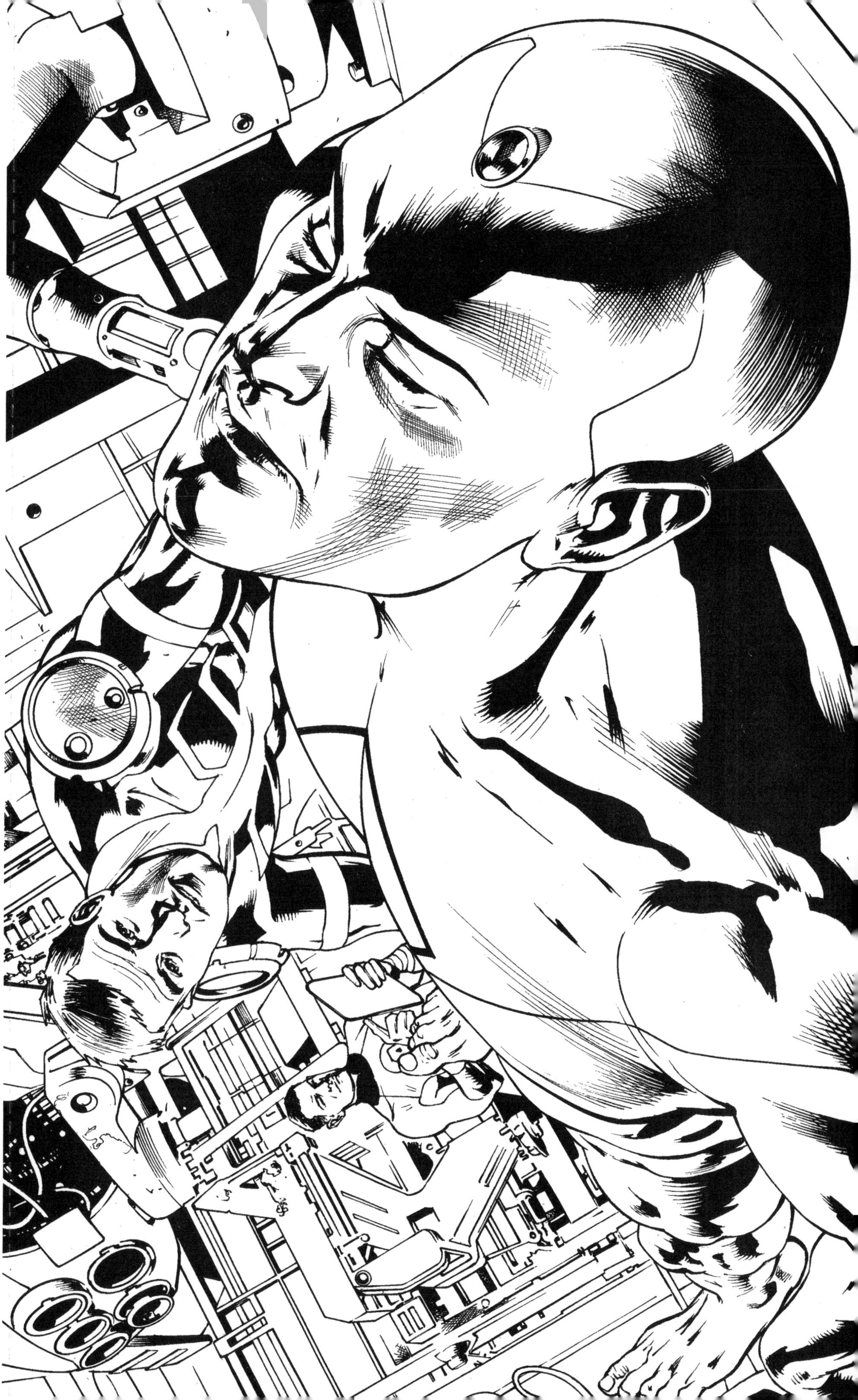

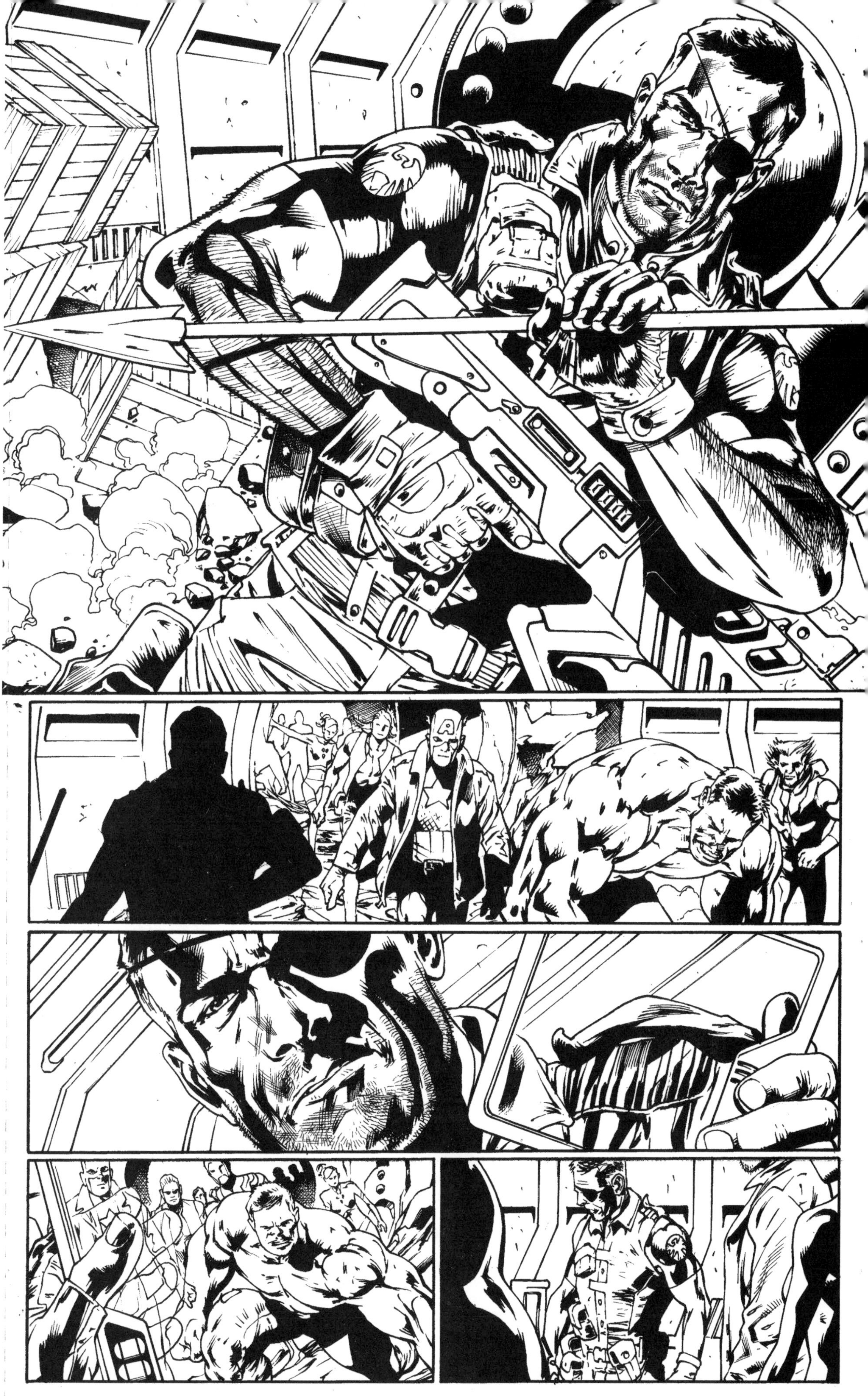

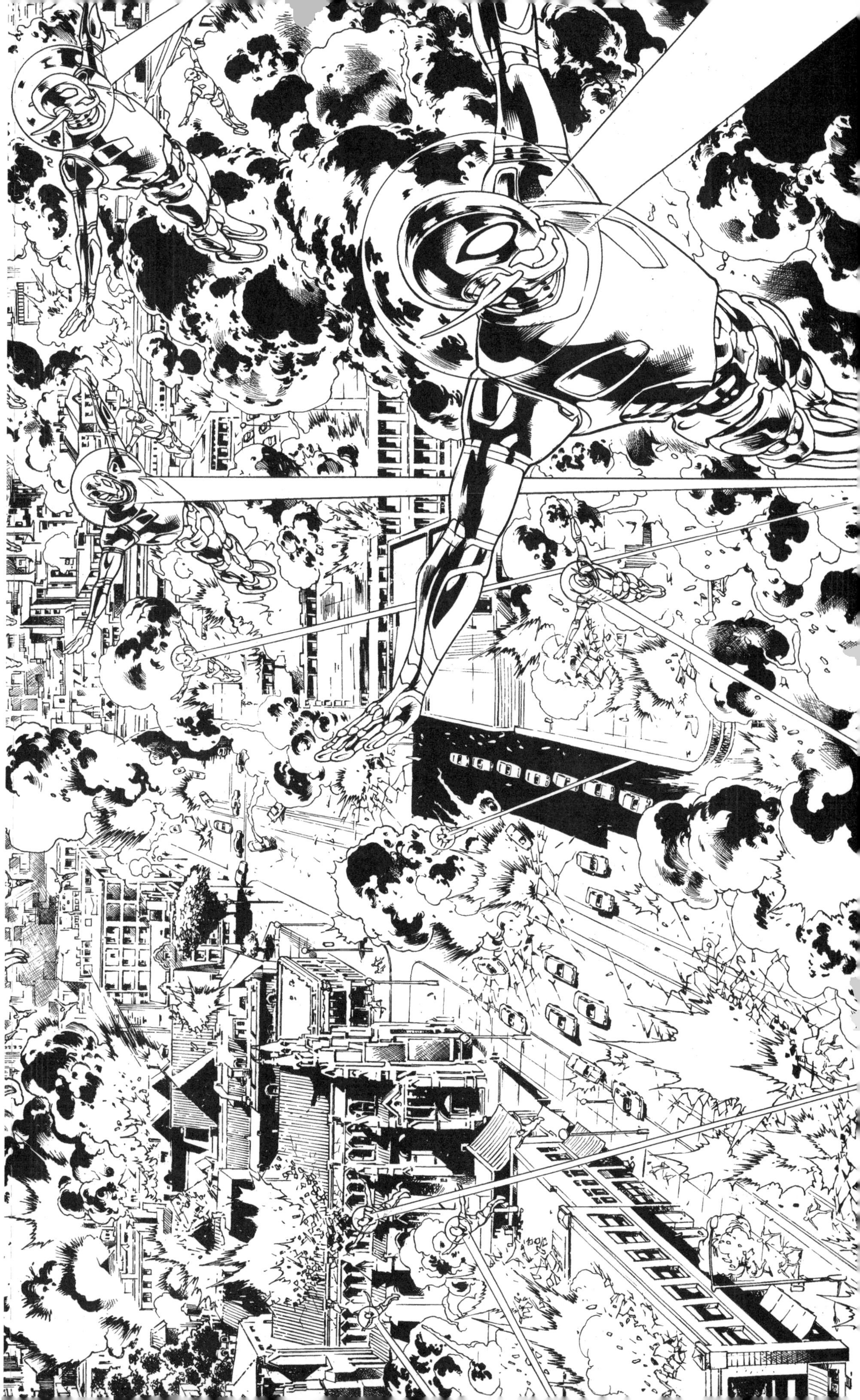

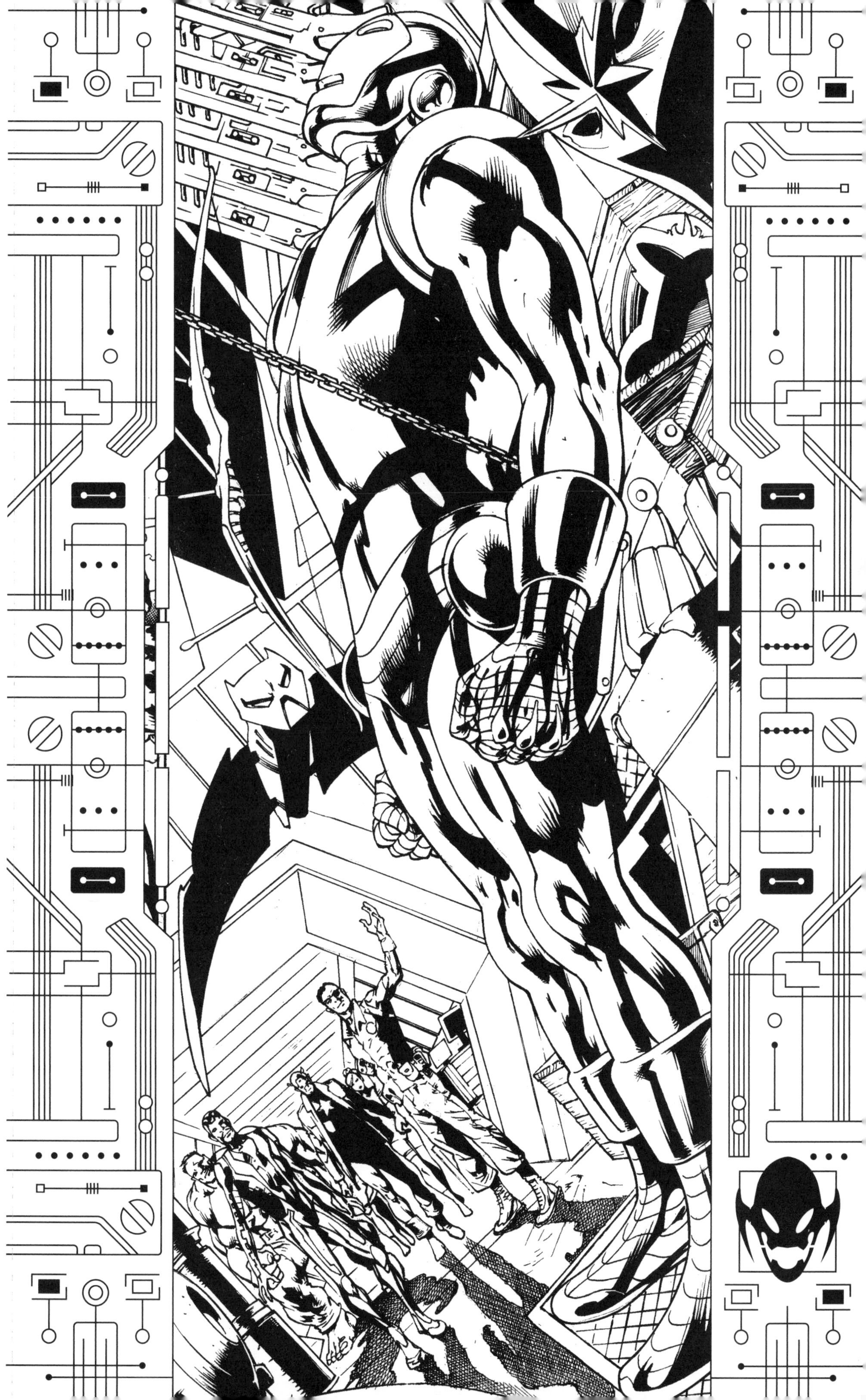

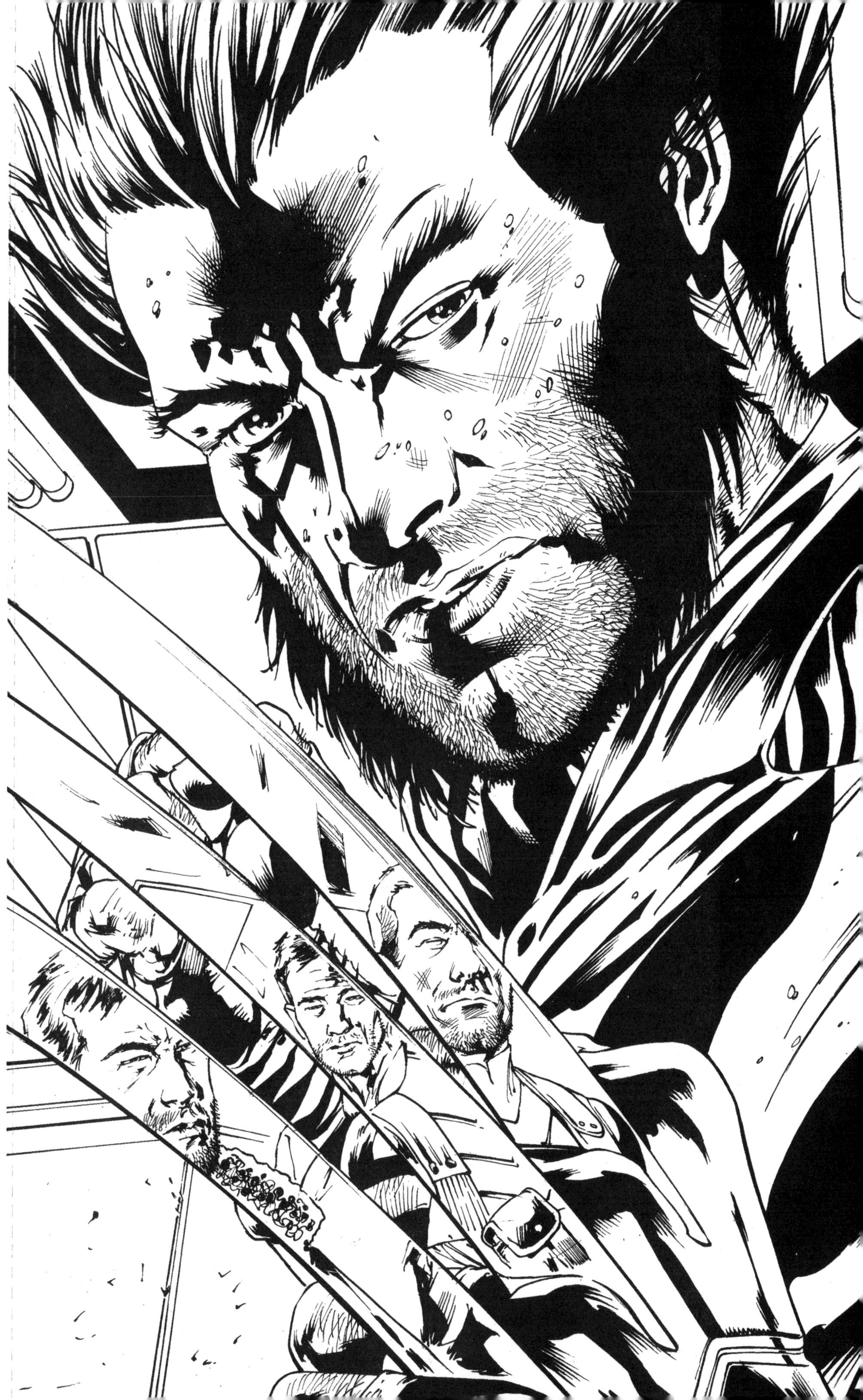

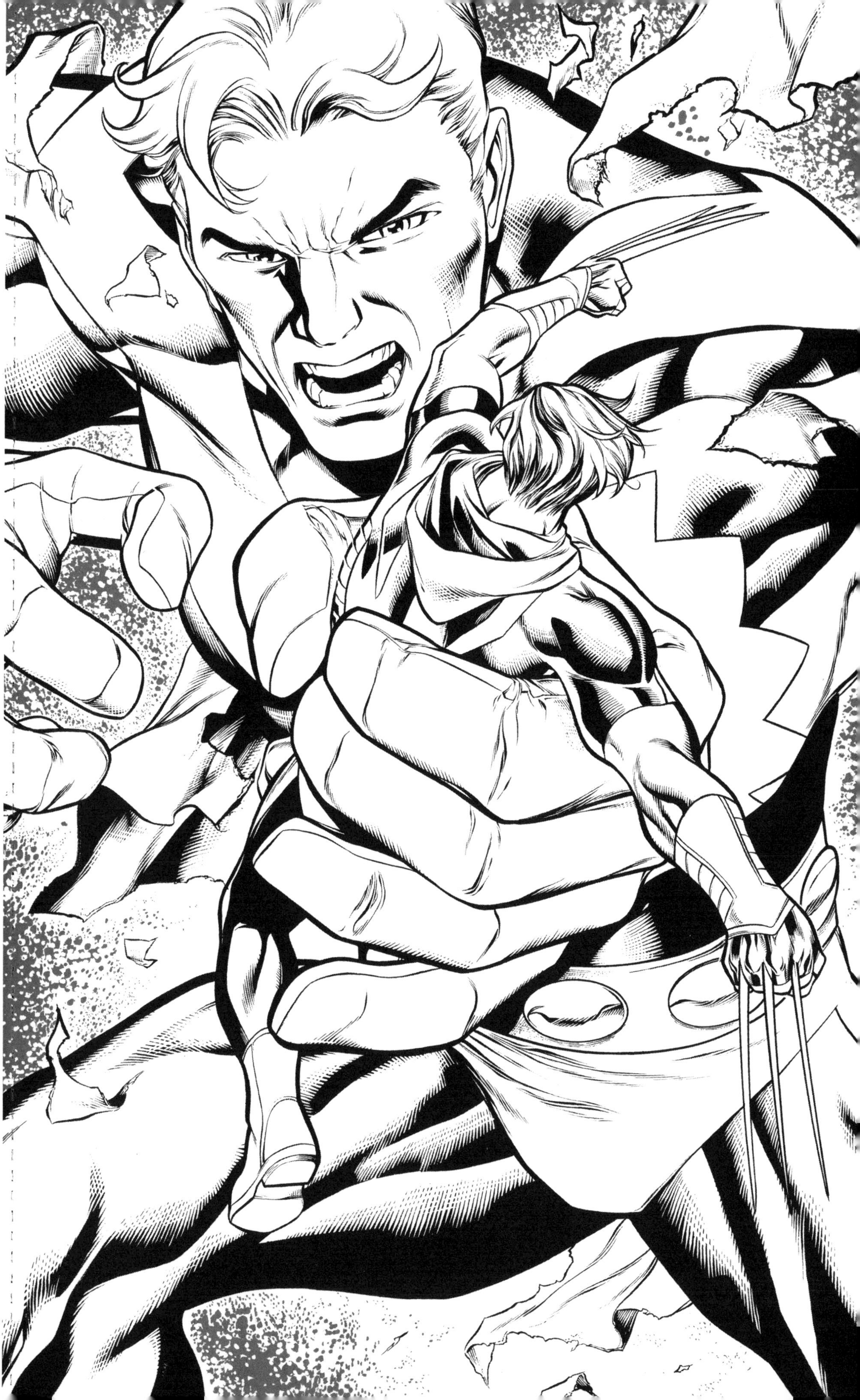

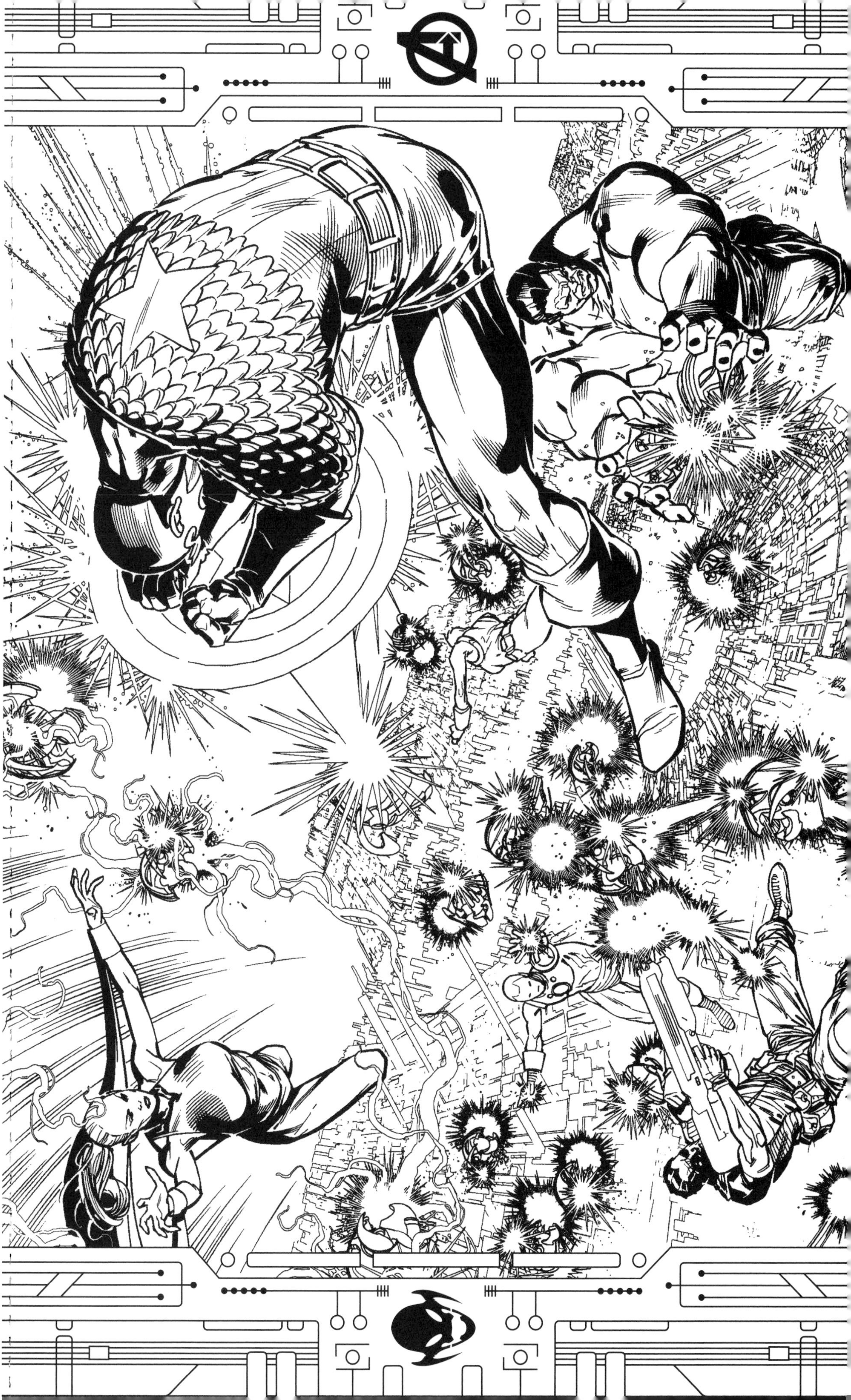

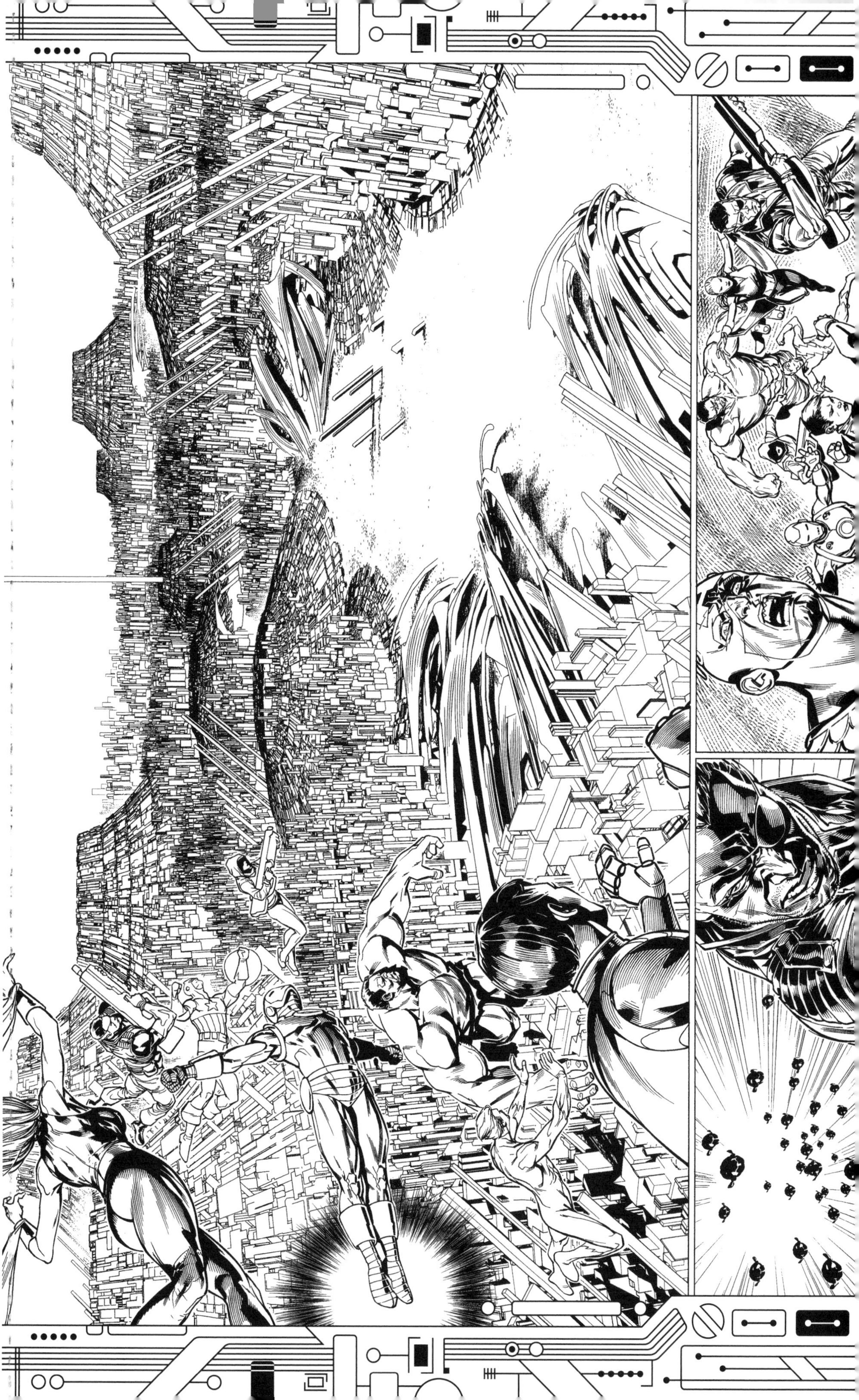

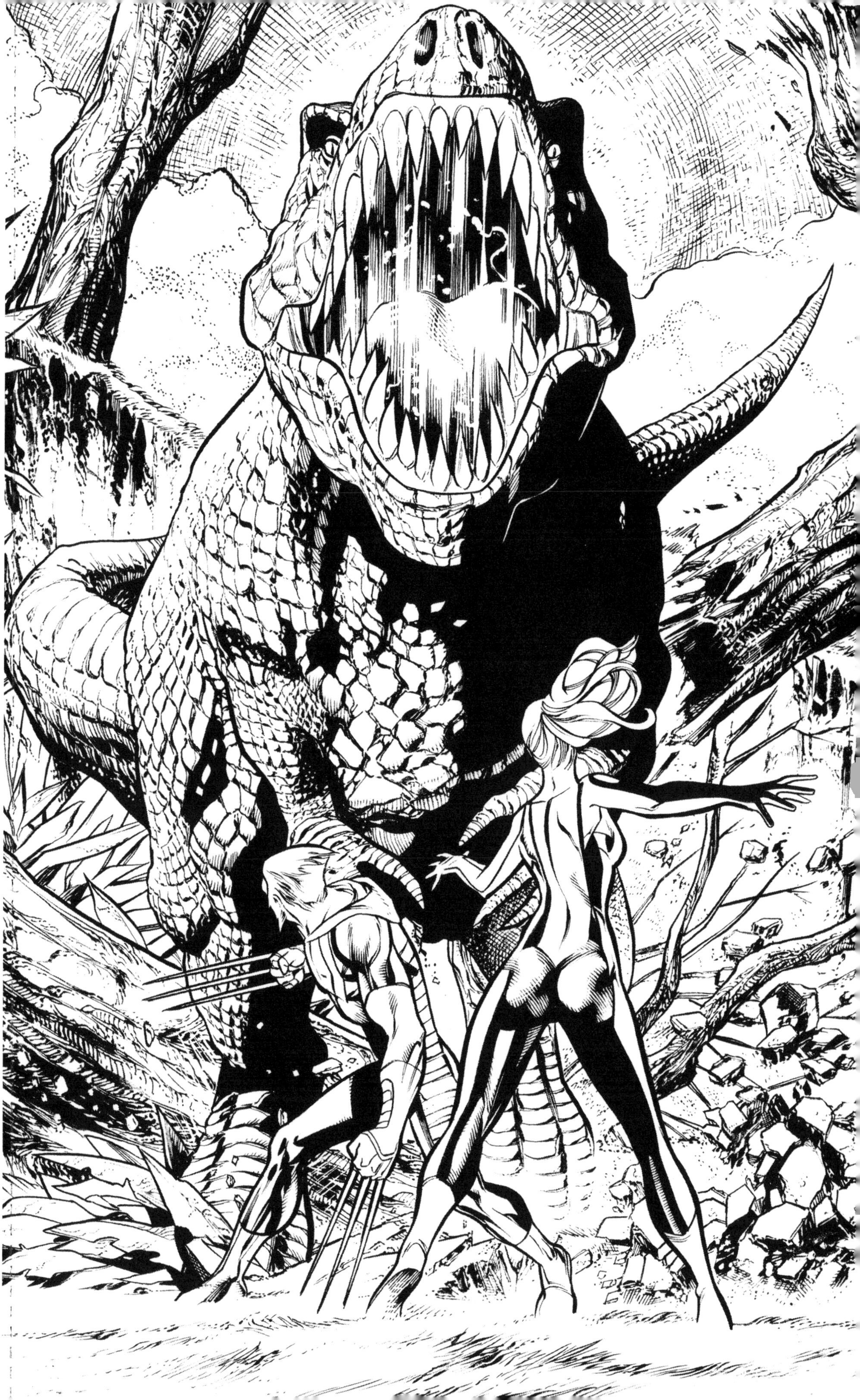

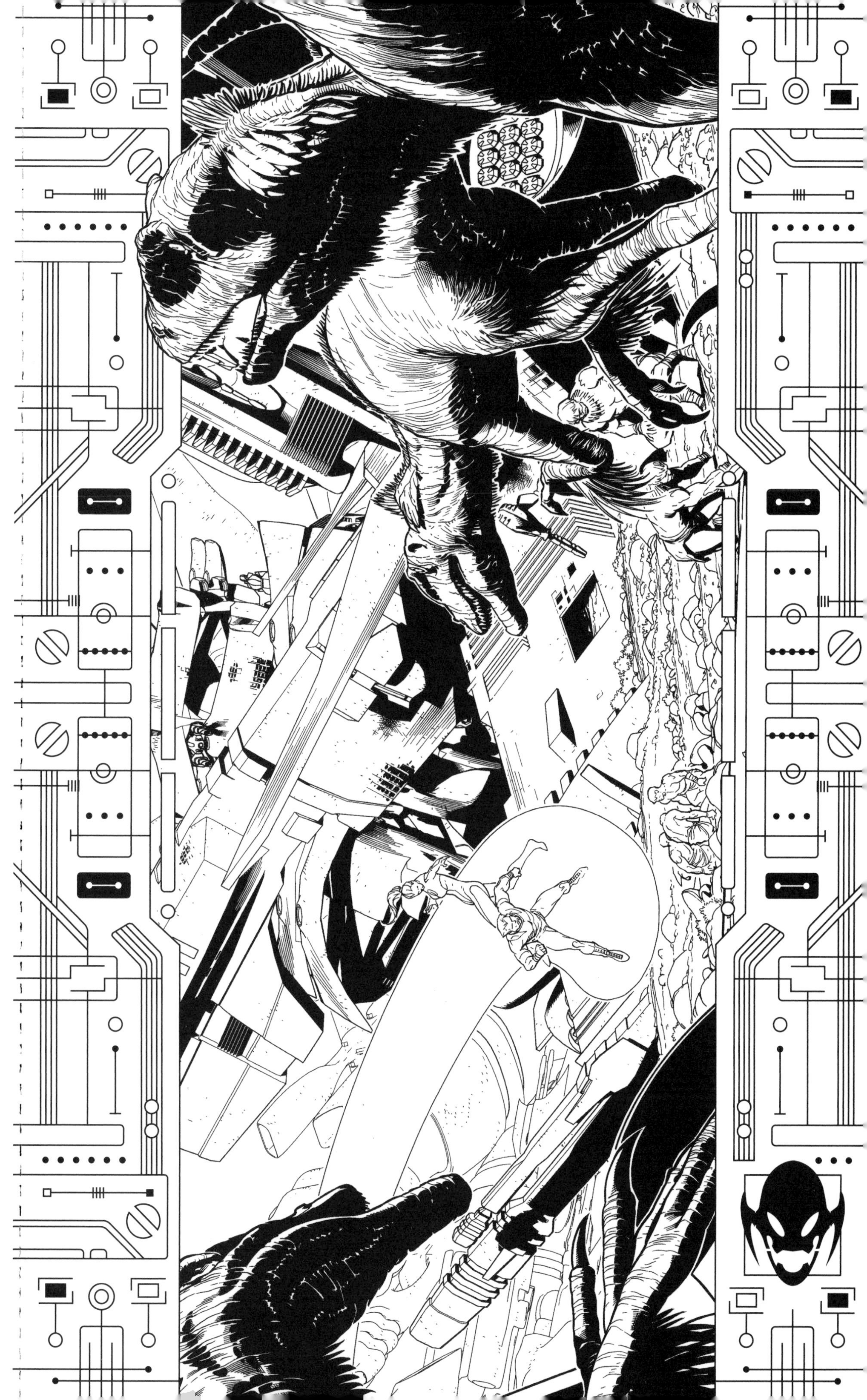

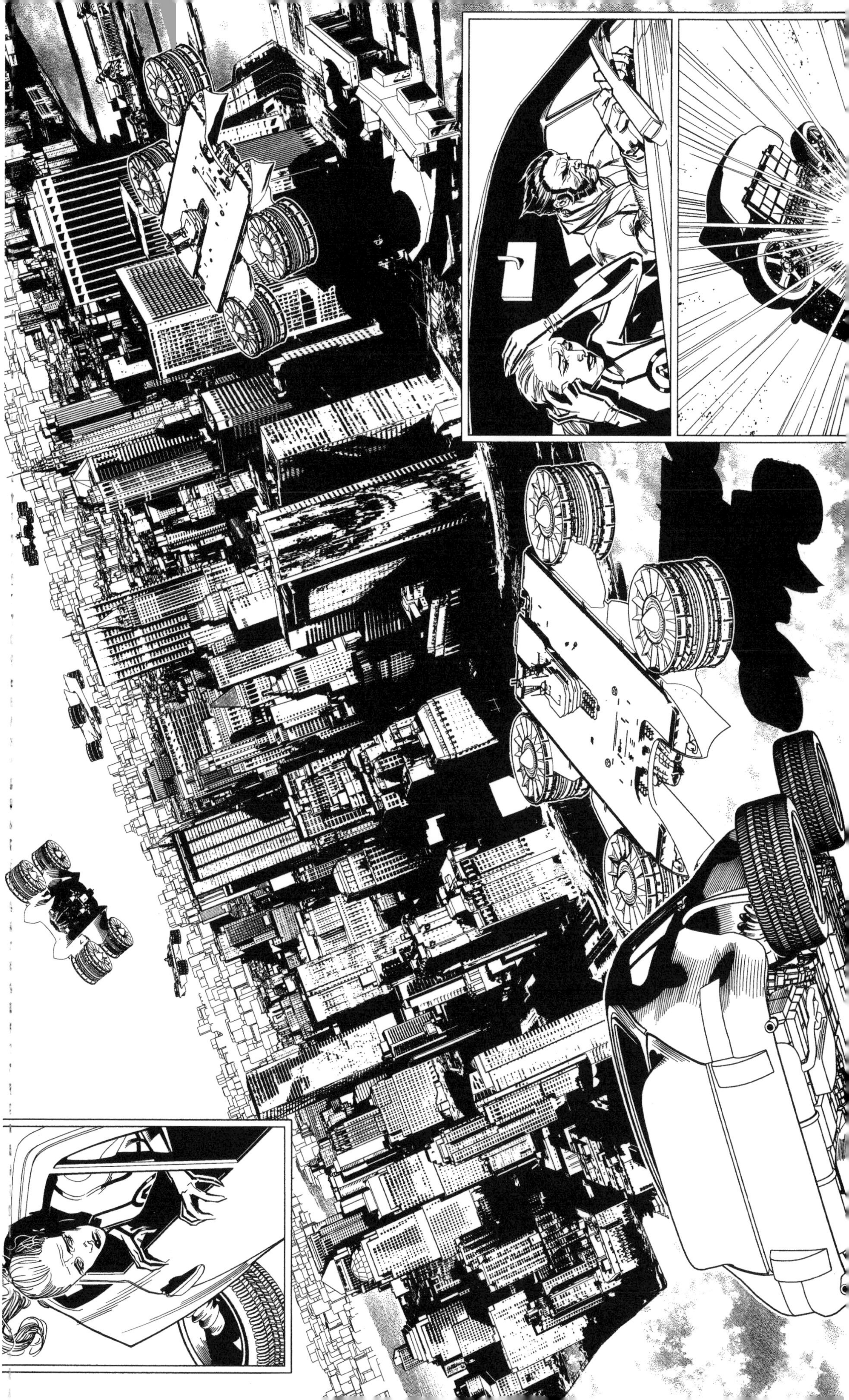

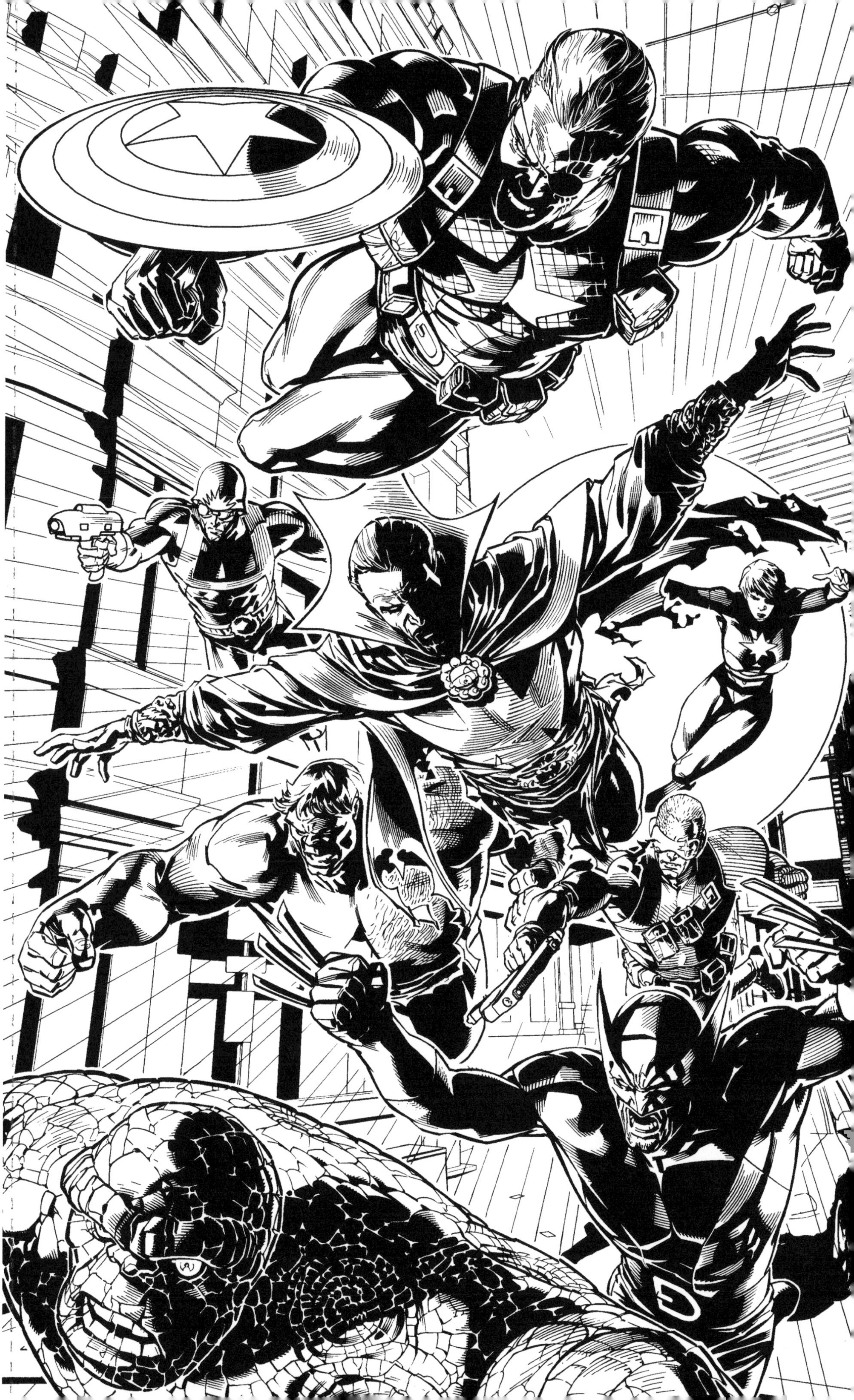

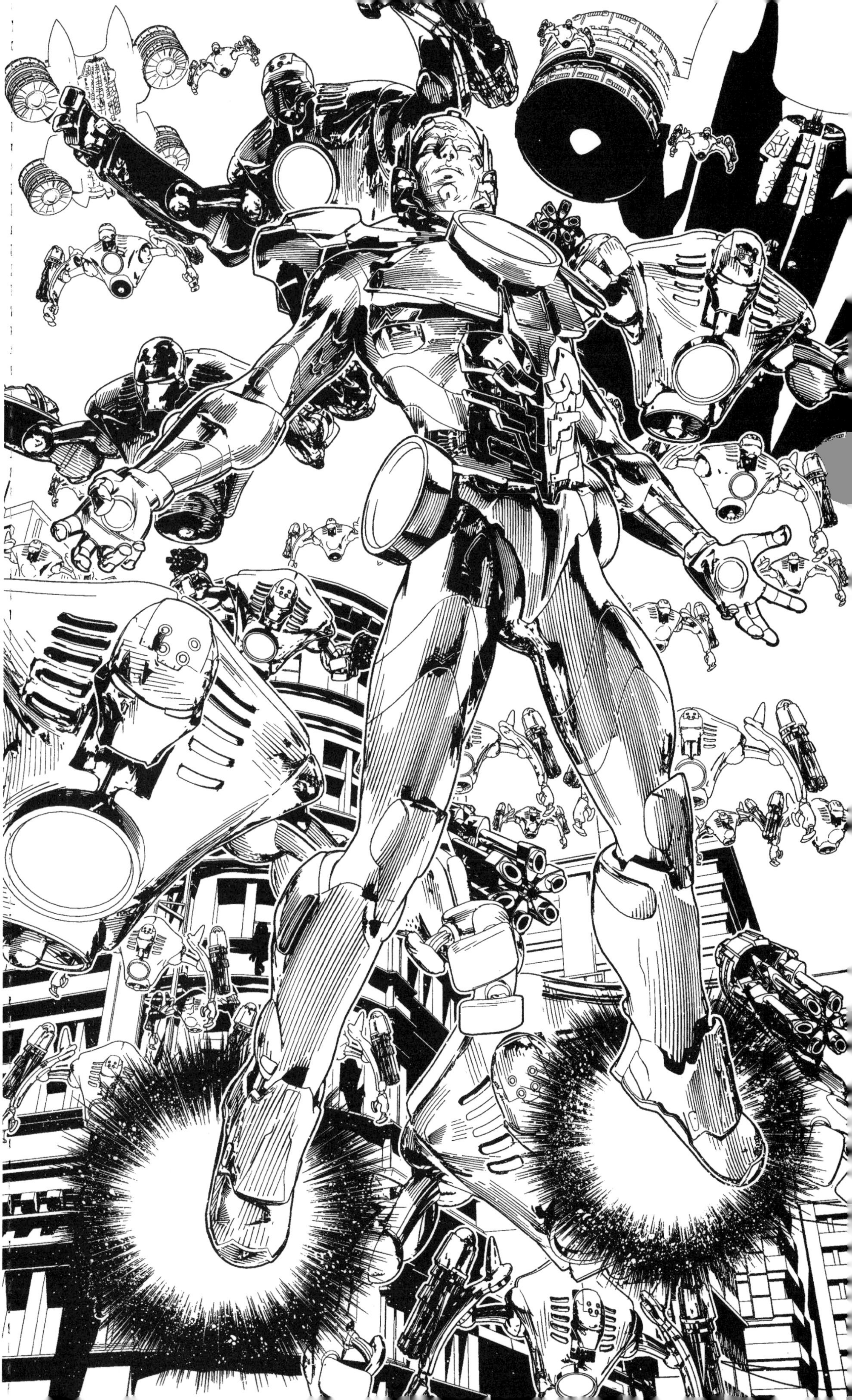

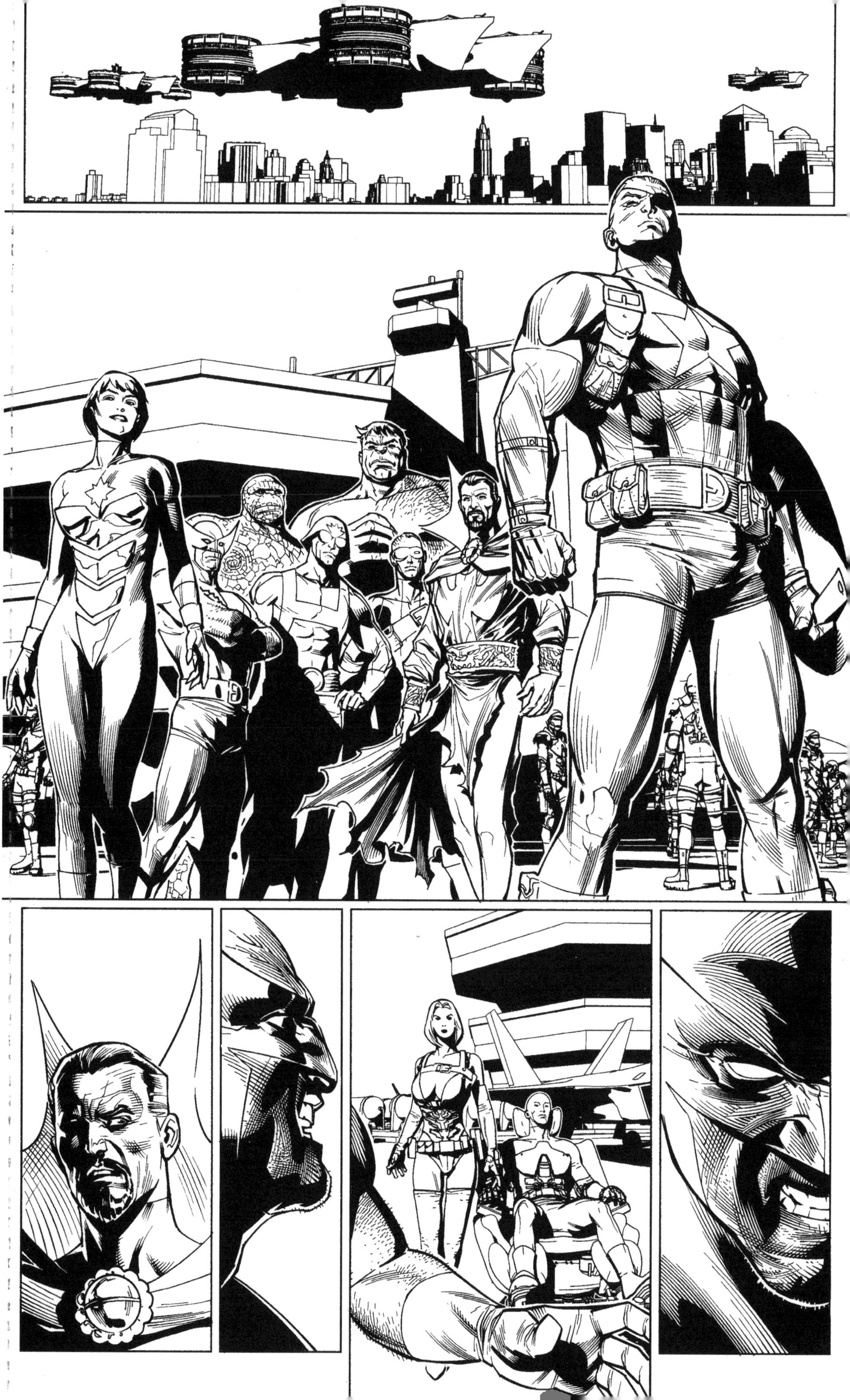

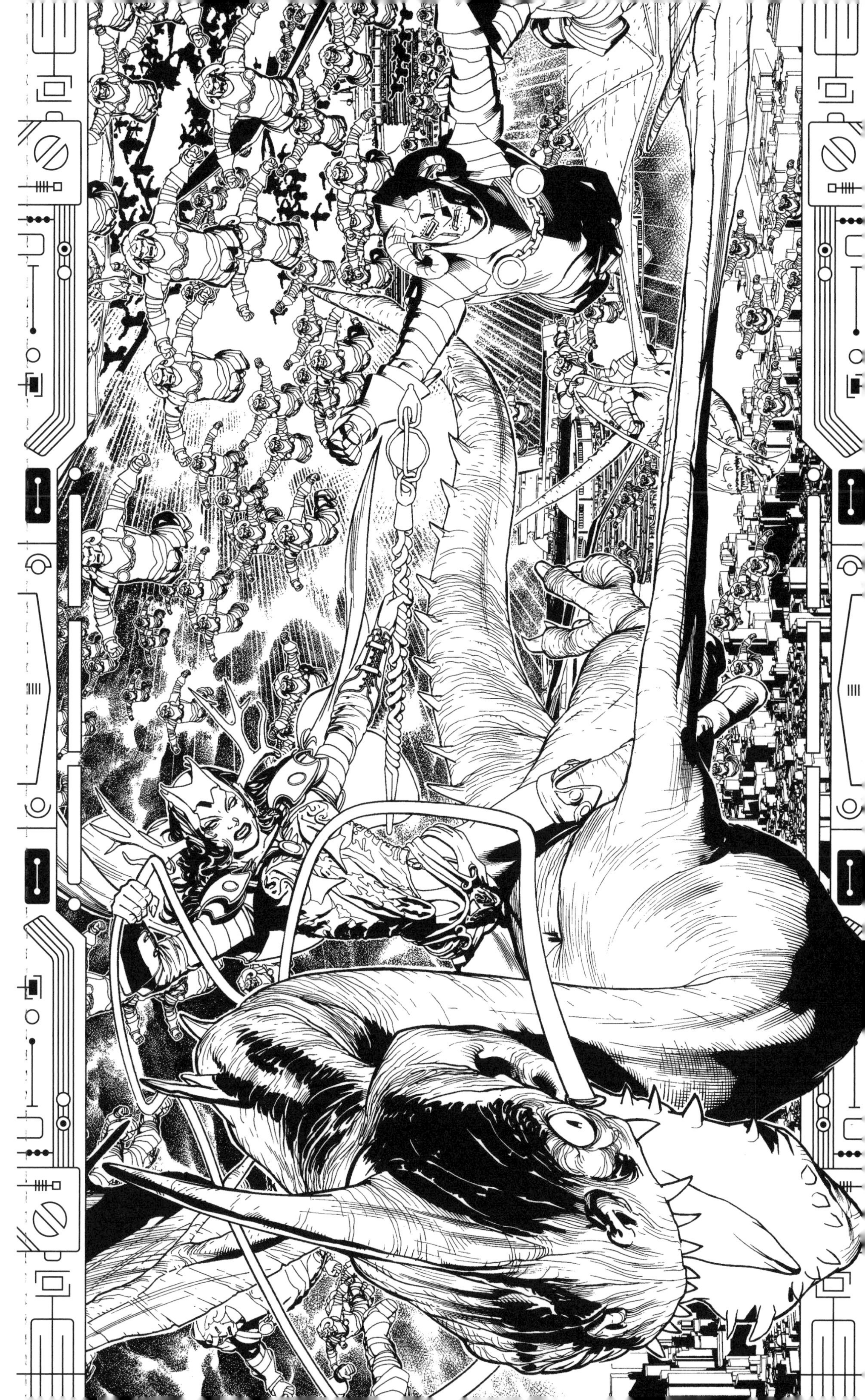

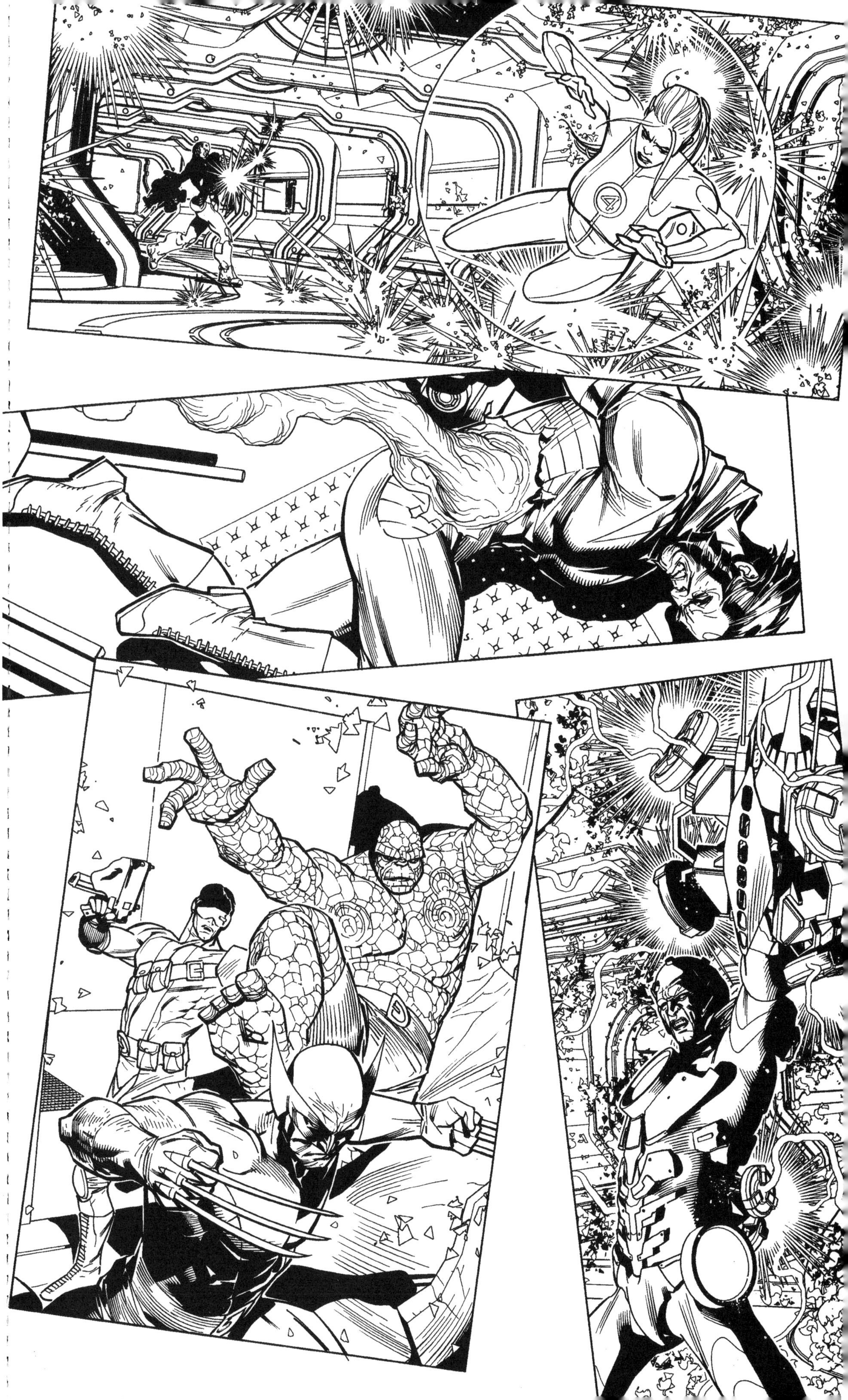

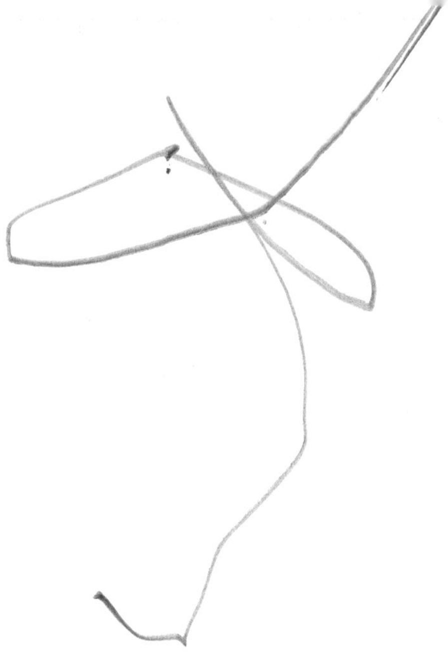

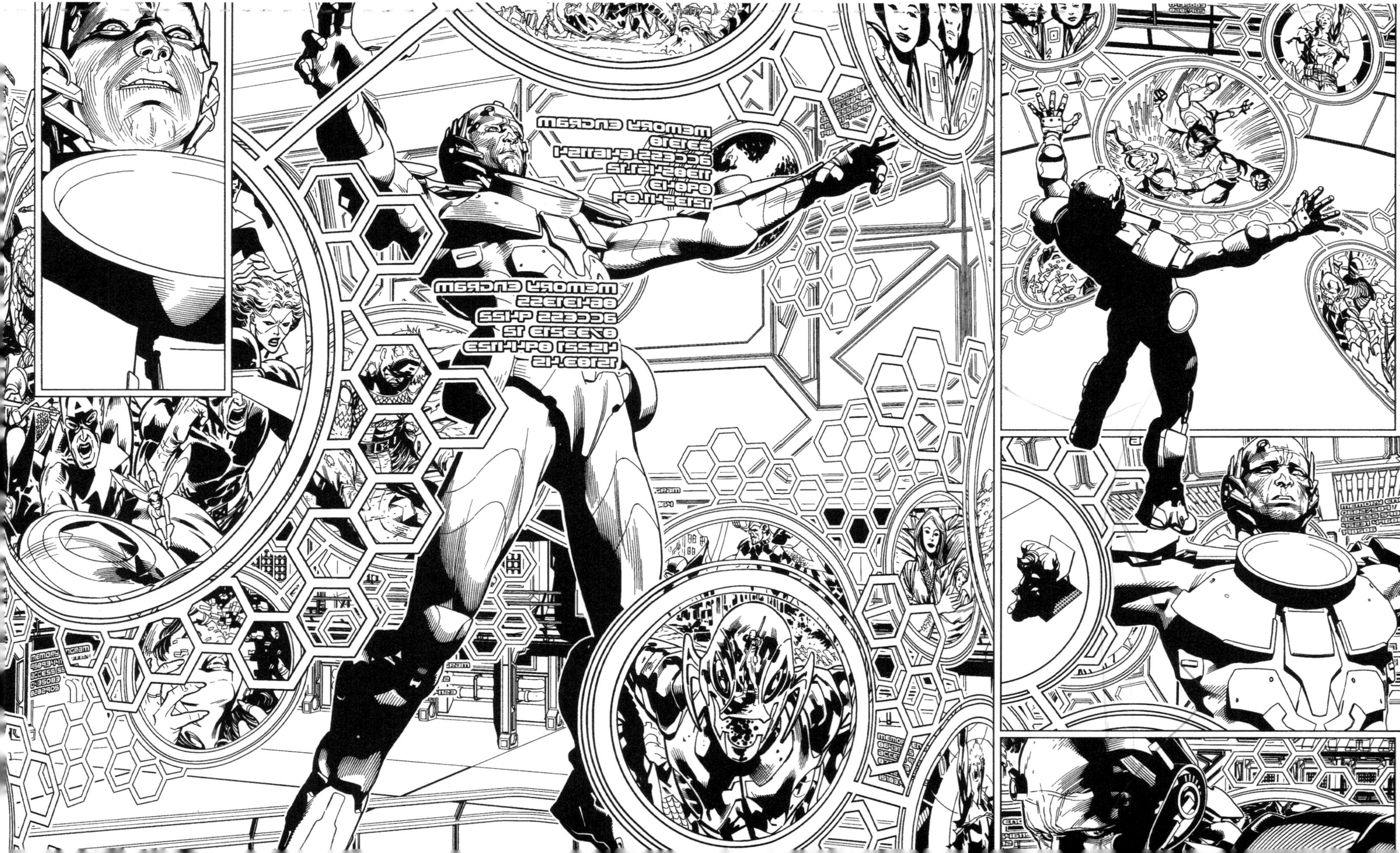

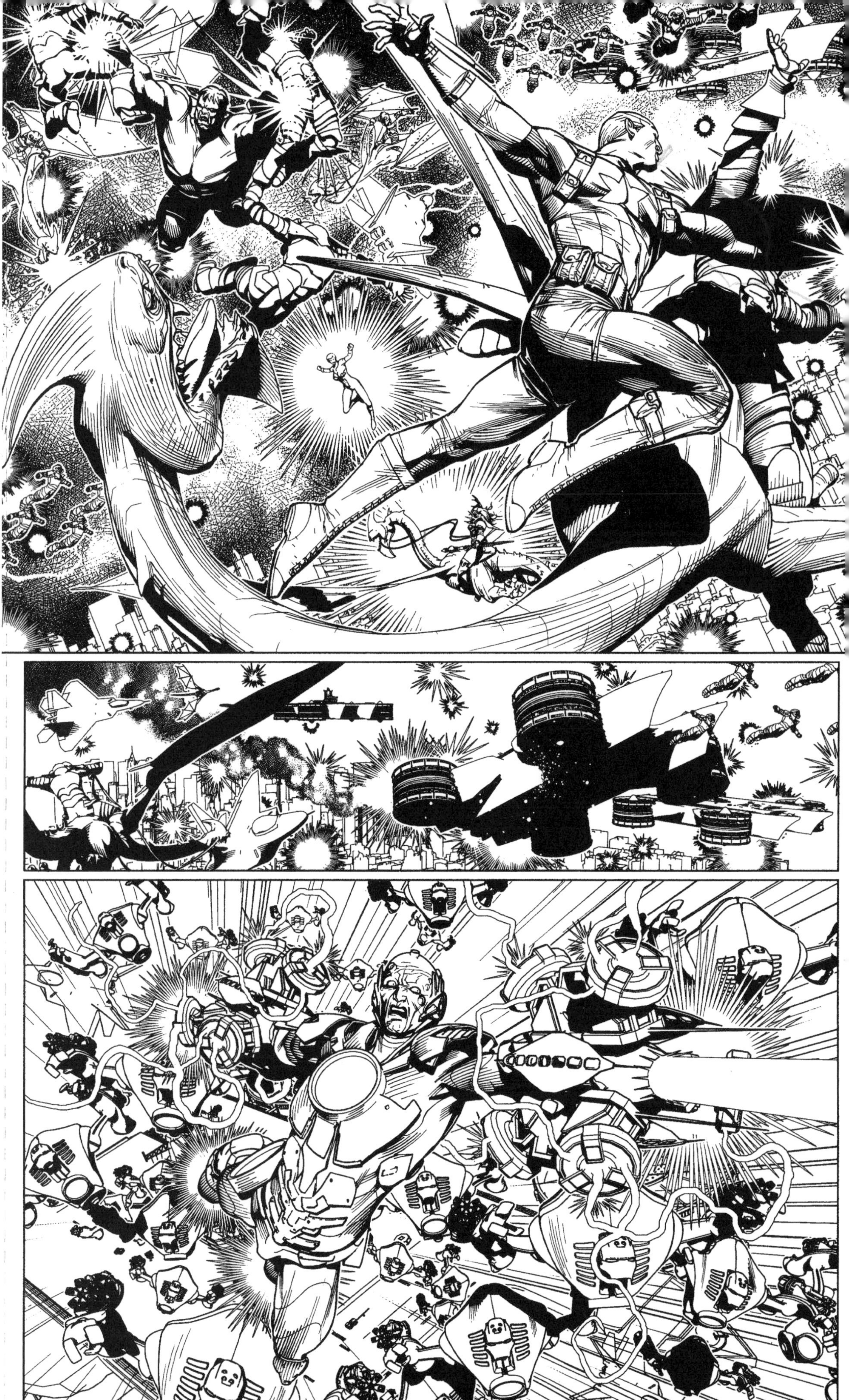

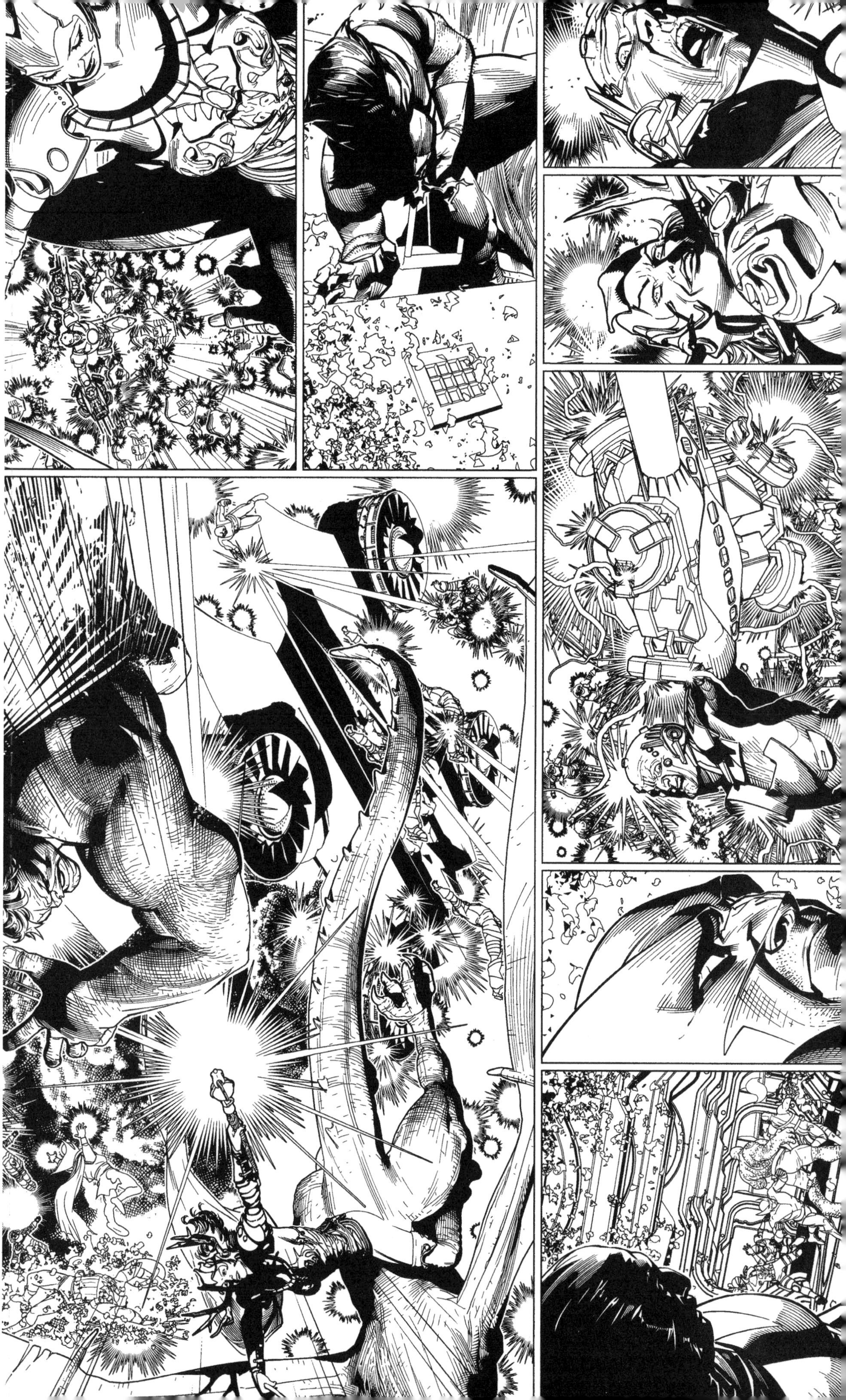

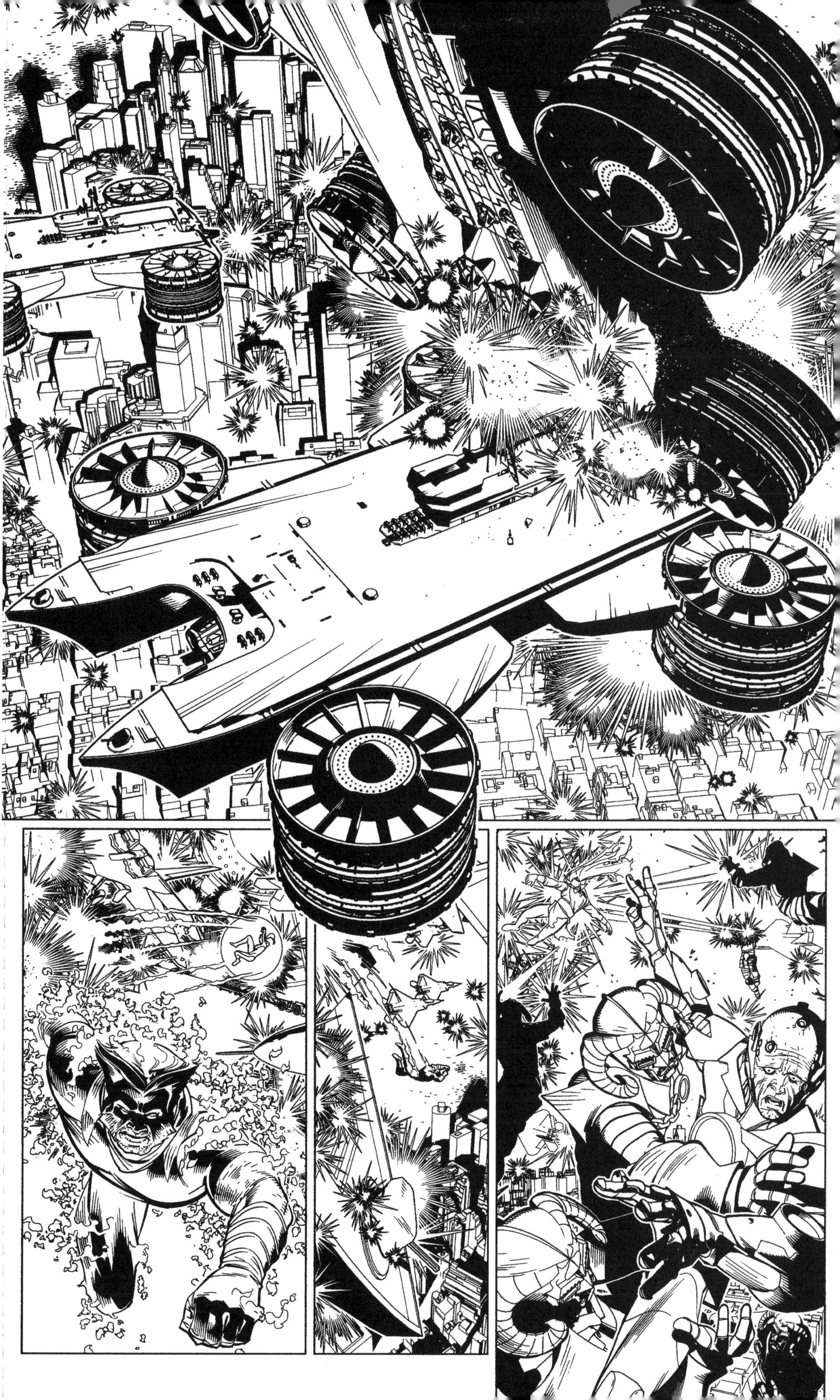

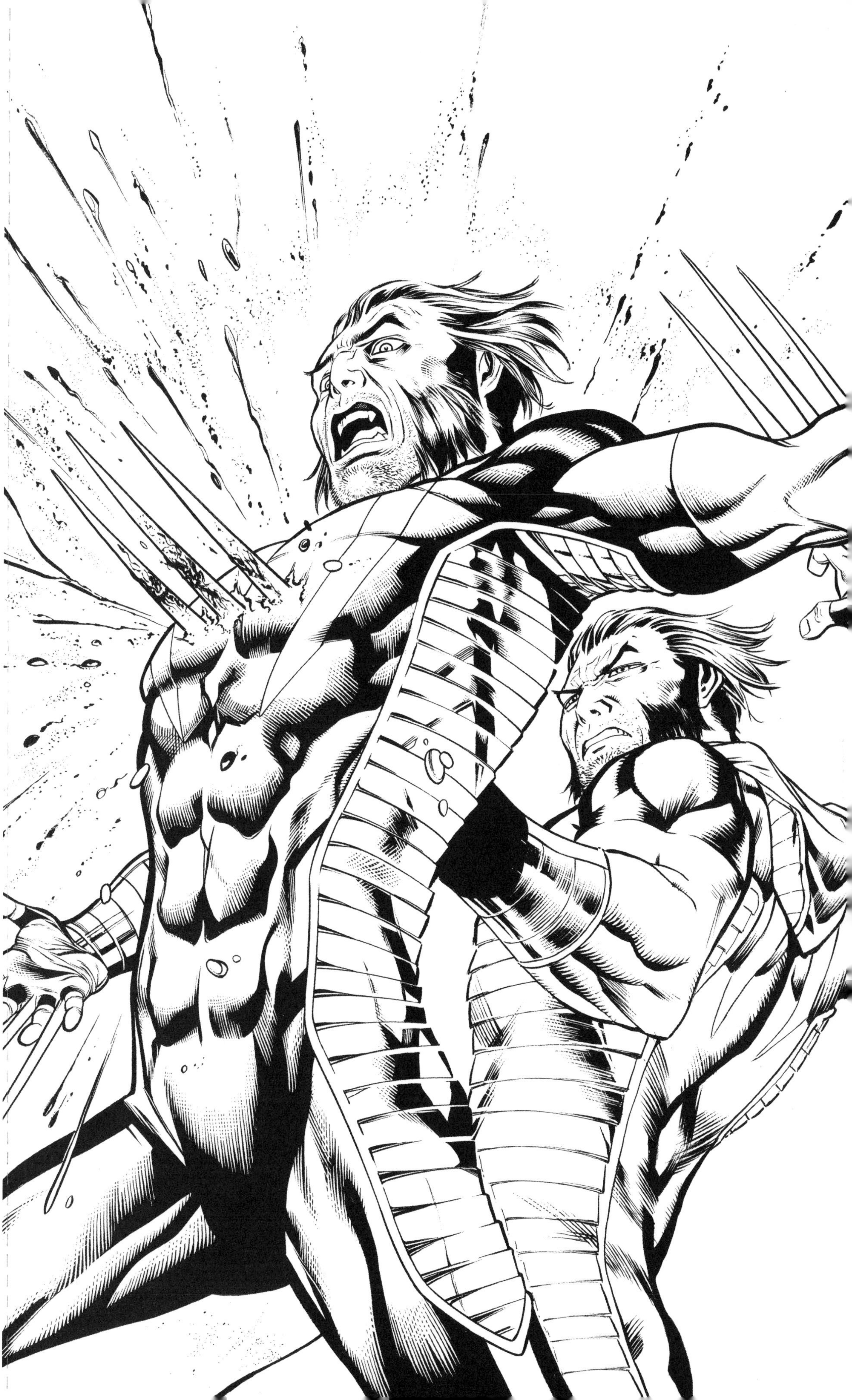

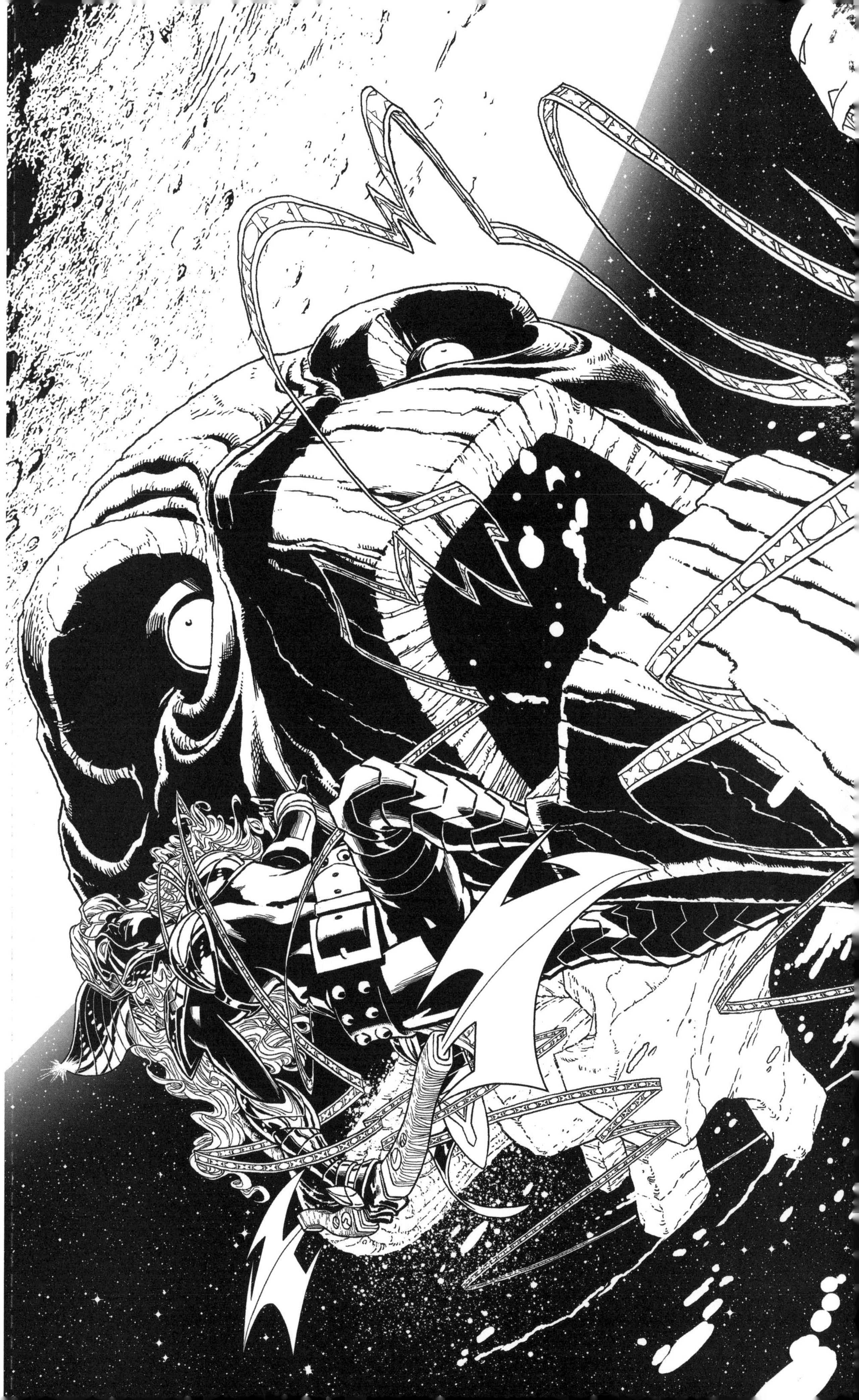

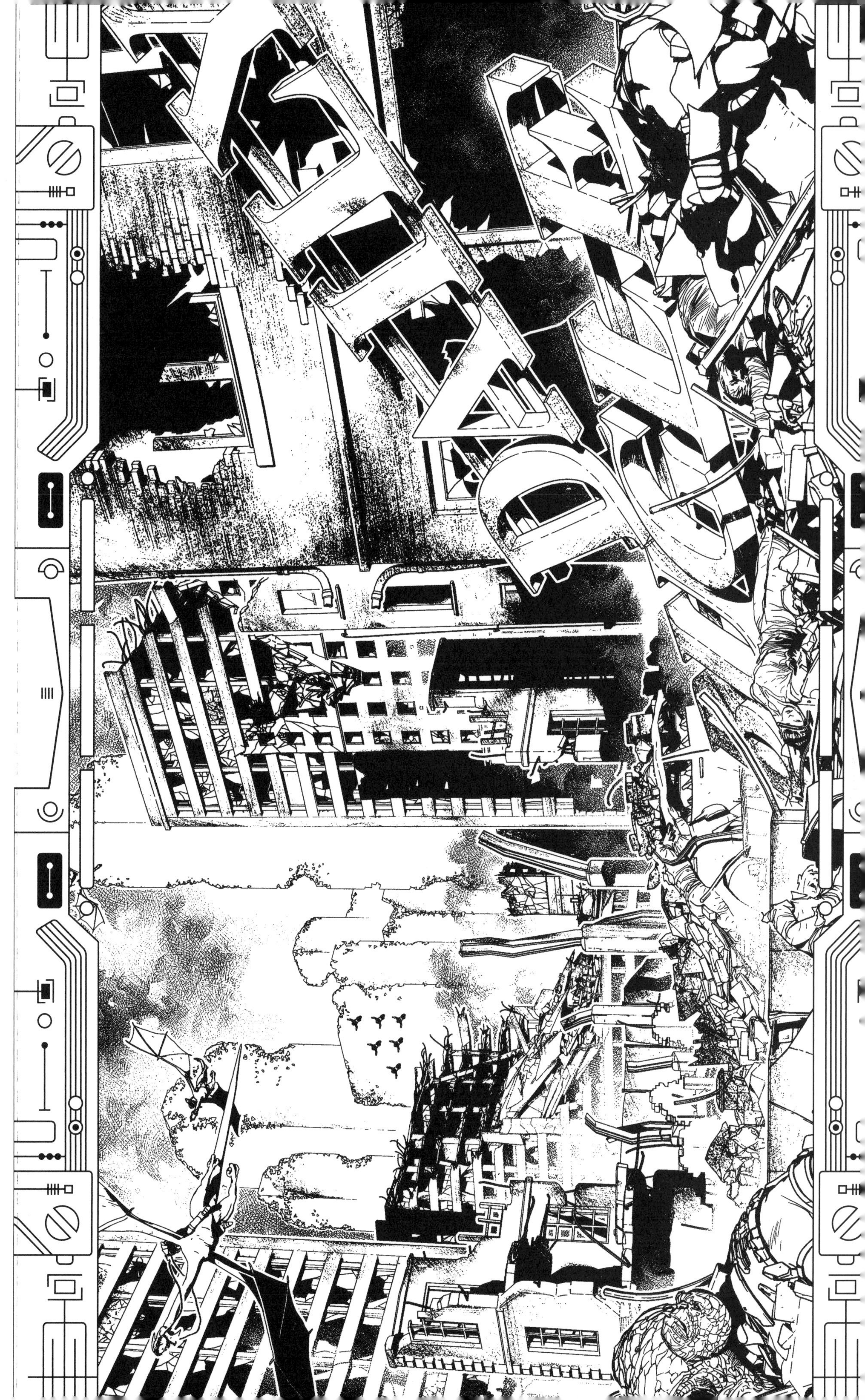

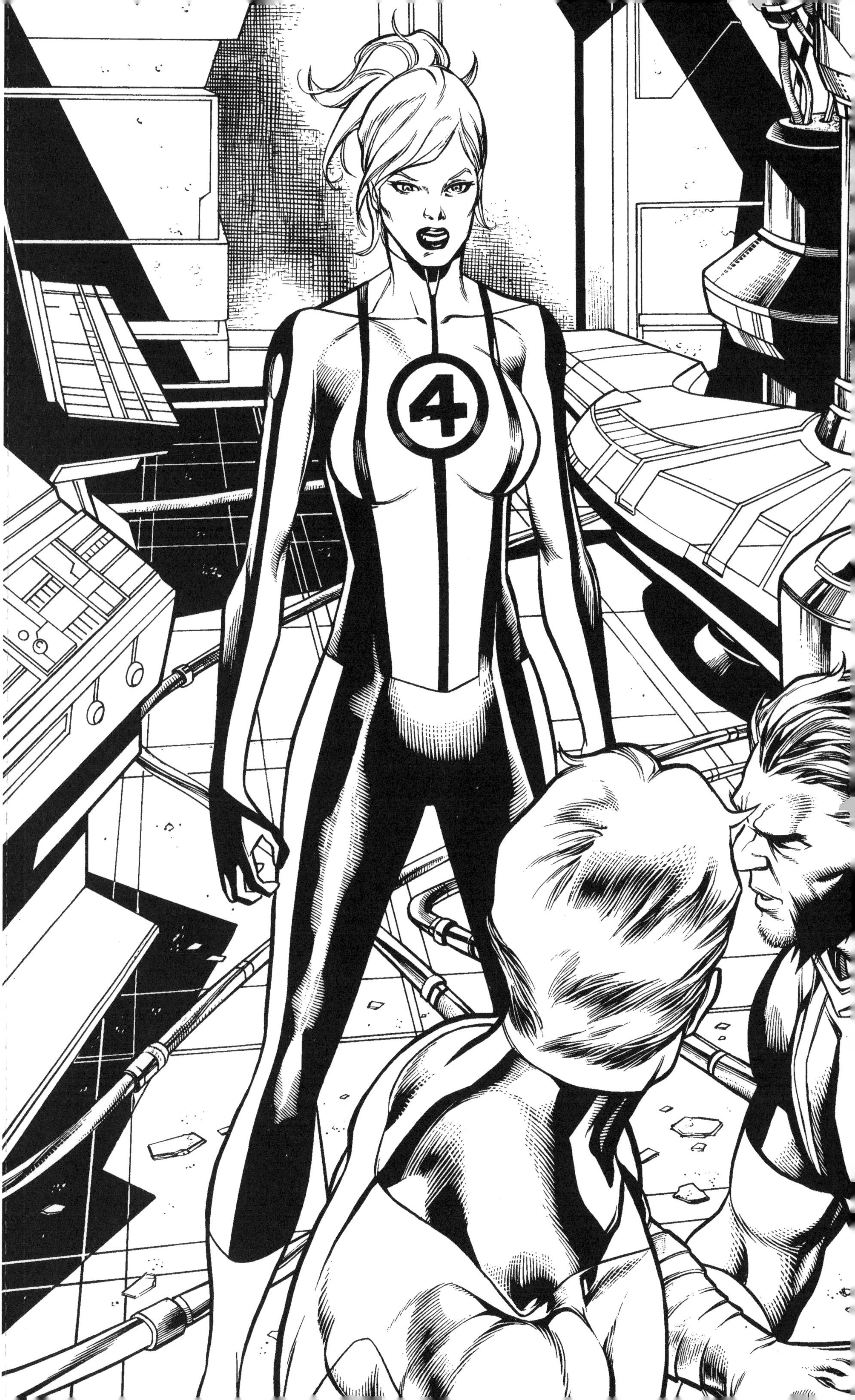

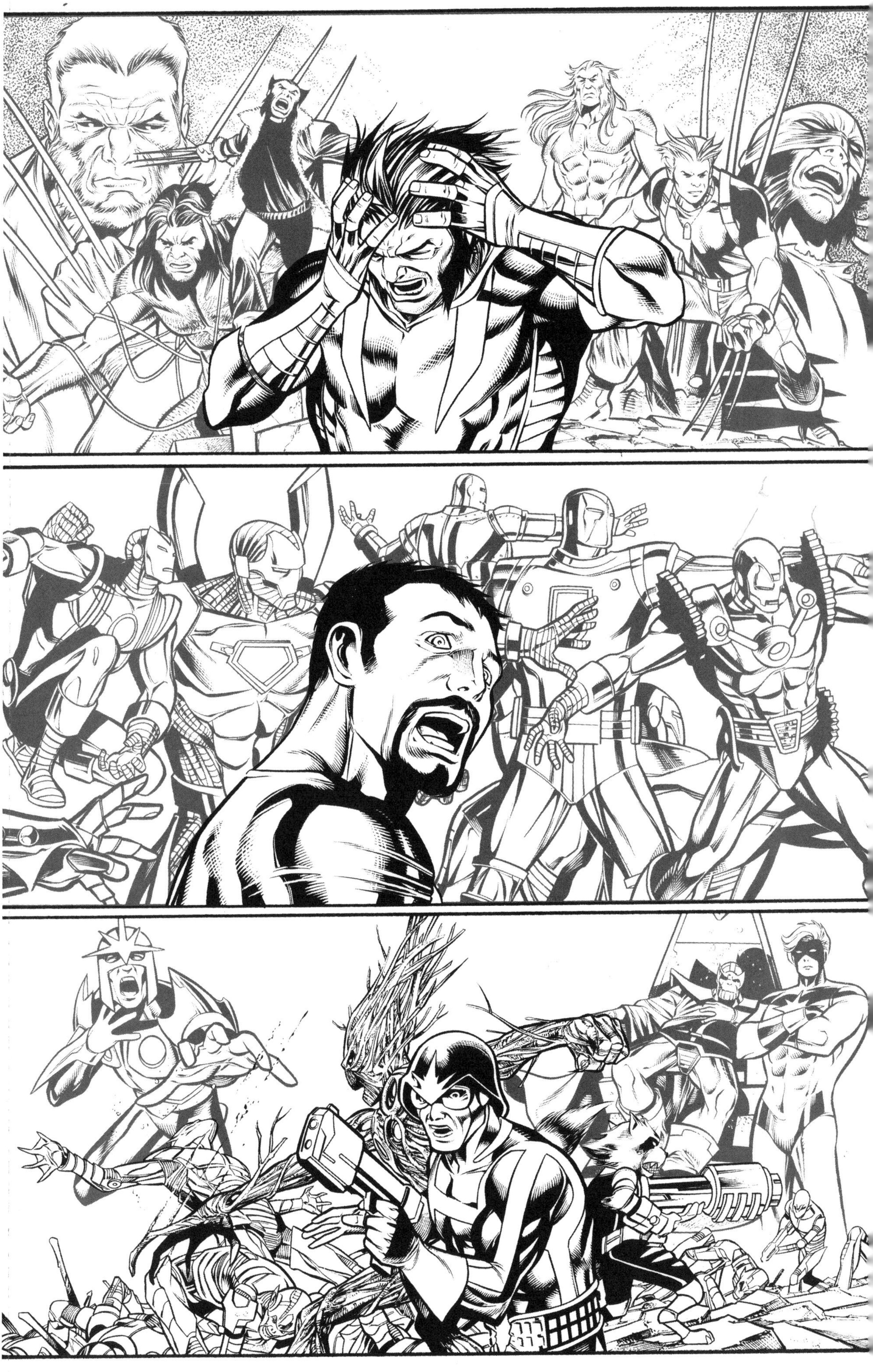

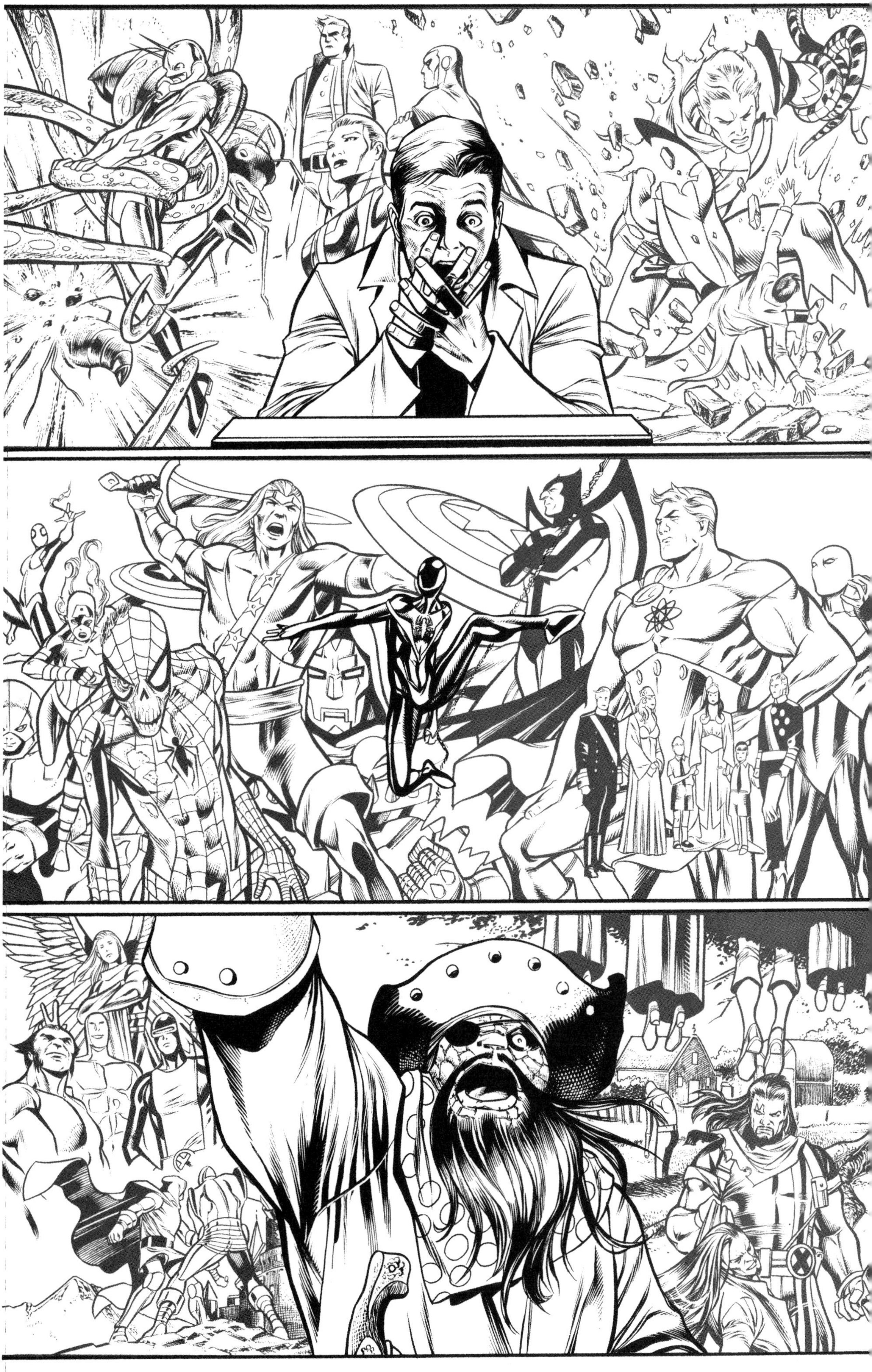

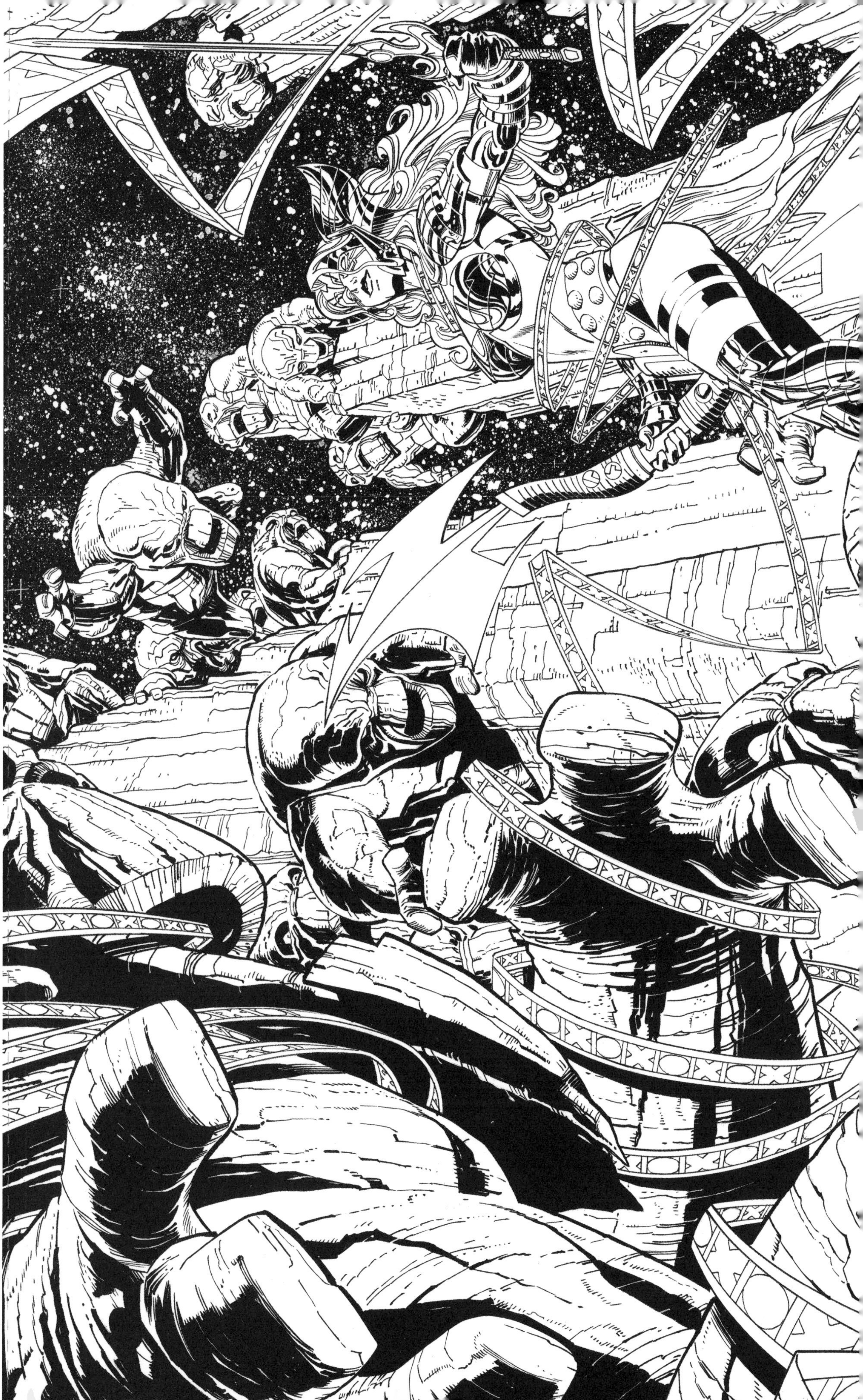

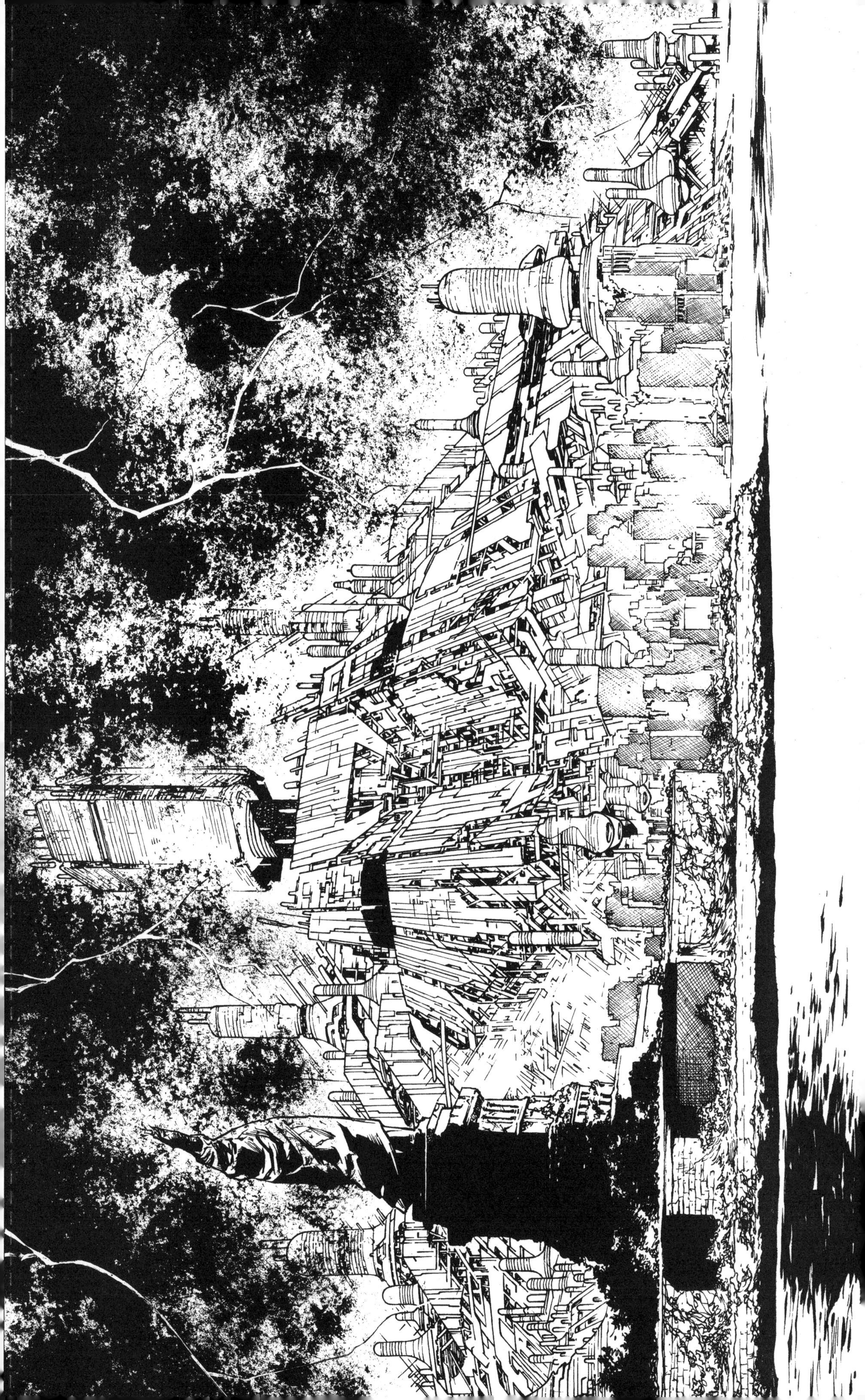